THOSE GREAT
MOVIE
ADS

THOSE GREAT MOVIE ADS

by Joe Morella
Edward Z. Epstein
and Eleanor Clark

Arlington House New Rochelle, New York

Library of Congress Catalog Card Number 75-189371

ISBN *0-87000-153-1*
MANUFACTURED IN THE UNITED STATES OF AMERICA

Designed by: James W. O'Bryan / Robert Bothell / Ultra Arts, Incorporated

Dedication

For our families and our great friend Jimmy Pearsall

Acknowledgments

The Diener Hauser Greenthal Co., Inc.
(With special thanks to Mr. Herbert Hauser)

Mal Barbour
Edwin Brodkin
Patrick B. Clark
Ernest Cunningham
The Echo Bookshop
David C. L'Heureux
Irving Ludwig
Duncan MacGregor
Nicholas Plattis
Dennis Preato
Arthur Manson
James W. O'Bryan
Philip Oppenheim
Al Poudell
Jonas Rosenfield, Jr.
Bob Smith
Evelyn Turner
Lou Valentino

Special thanks to Judith Crist
And grateful thanks to all the creative geniuses
who designed those great movie ads

Contents

Introduction

by Judith Crist

Movie stars and moguls may come, go and even fade away
forever from the film scene — but there will, as the old blurb line has it,
always be an ad man. From the first flicker of flicks to the last gasp of
cinema, the pitch will come with the picture and the old "Hello,
sucker!" will lure the boobs to the balcony.

But even the most cynical and the most cineastic among us are
willing to face the fact that flackery is an essence of show biz, that we
are all, somehow, customers of the big sell and that we've salivated in
Pavlovian hound-dog fashion at the first trumpetings of things to come
in Shadowland.

My movie-going generation was not, I must confess, conditioned by
newspaper ads. Children of Loew's Paradise, we were lured back to
our double features-cum-shorts, featurettes, newsreels and trailers by
the glorious multi-colored posters (pre-Technicolor colorful and huge
reproductions, often, of those relatively minuscule black-and-white
movie-page ads) and by the titillations of the coming attractions, those
raucous sense-ripping taste-defying incoherencies that captured the
crux of the come-on, if not the fine points of the film that was being
touted. And as we outgrew our Saturday-matinee ration and expanded
our movie-going to the all-American high of twice and even thrice a
week, the impetus was to catch the movies we had not seen — so
undiscriminating was our passion. But we doted on the ads as
enhancement, saved them for the photos and drawings of the stars,
for the blarneyed sloganization of what we had seen — from G.W.T.W.
to the Gable-Garson catch, to that perpetual "Together Again!"
teamsmanship of Jimmie Dunne and Sally Eilers, Spencer Tracy and

Introduction

Katharine Hepburn, Dick Powell and Ruby Keeler, Bogey-Lorre and Greenstreet, Tarzan and the Apes and/or Jane, Wallace Beery and Marie Dressler, Judy Garland and Mickey Rooney. And from there on to the purple-prose gardens, abloom with lush items like *"Irresistible* their love! INESCAPABLE their fears!" for Bergman and Peck in *Spellbound* and, for Burton and Taylor in *The Sandpiper*, "From the beginning, they knew it was wrong . . . ", which might also be noted as a prime example of the self-criticism often inherent in the best of movie blurbs.

But what is a film critic doing admitting to a passion for the sludge side of movies — a sludge that has assumed a gloss, a sophistication and even on occasion a touch of lyricism in the graphics of recent years? (I am thinking of the heartwarming eloquence of Saul Bass's old man and child as the colophon for *The Two of Us;* the hard-hatted hard-hitting target design, photograph and urge to "Keep America Beautiful" for *Joe;* the haunting allure of the multi-magnified butterfly for *The Hellstrom Chronicle* and the queasy thrill for the rat of *Willard.* I am trying to forget the imbecility of "Love means never having to say you're sorry" for *Love Story,* replete with Ryan O'Neal and Ali MacGraw, that was reduced to its proper level with parallel photos of the unmasked horror of Vincent Price clutching fair maiden for *The Abominable Dr. Phibes* with the declaration that "Love means never having to say you're ugly.")

Introduction

After all, like the farmer and the cowboy, the critic and the movie ad man have become reputed natural-born enemies since we entered, relatively early on, into the era of the quote ad. For some of the smaller critical fry, the movie company's touting of their favorable words in other publications via ads has provided publicity, stature and ego-massage. But more often critics, large-circulation and small, have suffered at the hands of quote seekers. The sins of omission, deletion and sheer perversion of meanings by excerpting reached a recent peak that resulted in New York City's Commissioner of Consumer Affairs taking a hand and working out fair-play rules for critics' quotes. And if indeed quote ads have any value, it is as often to inform by sheer omission of certain critics' names and phrases just what the appeal of a film is. When the sponsors resort to the Hickstown Gazette or the London Monthly Cinema Blab for the good word, those who pay heed to quote ads get the message.

But in the last analysis, sad for a critic to concede, it's the producer's "sell" that sells a film and the word-of-mouth that sends folks to the box-office, on the premise that "they" said the movie was a good one. And who are "they"? A friend, a relative, a critic — or an ad man? Sweet mystery of motivation . . . let it never be finally resolved. Let the ads flourish as part of the mystery, part of the mystique and a very large part of the movie mythology on which we thrive.

INGRID BERGMAN
GREGORY PECK

ALFRED HITCHCOCK'S

SPELLBOUND

Doris DAY   James CAGNEY

YOU'LL LOVE IT!

The Musical Masterpiece of the Year!

LOVE ME OR LEAVE ME

CinemaScope

Photographed in EASTMAN COLOR

co-starring CAMERON MITCHELL

with ROBERT KEITH TOM TULLY

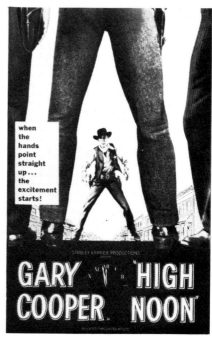

when the hands point straight up... the excitement starts!

GARY COOPER in 'HIGH NOON'

Darryl F. Zanuck presents

OLIVIA de HAVILLAND in

the Snake Pit

also Starring

MARK STEVENS and LEO GENN

with Celeste Holm · Glenn Langan

and Helen Craig · Leif Erickson · Beulah Bondi · Lee Patrick · Howard Freeman
Natalie Schafer · Ruth Donnelly · Katherine Locke · Frank Conroy · Minna Gombell

Produced by ANATOLE LITVAK and ROBERT BASSLER

Screen Play by Frank Partos and Millen Brand · Based on the Novel by Mary Jane Ward

Directed by ANATOLE LITVAK

20th CENTURY-FOX

She knows all about Love-potions and Lovely Motions!

CINEMA GUILD presents

Veronica does strange things to men. Like appearing in their homes at midnight. Or breaking up their weddings to other girls. Or making them love her — even when they don't want to. Yes sir, when this 1942 witch charms 'em — brother, they stay charmed!

"I MARRIED A WITCH"

"She's got him so he doesn't know which is witch!"

STARRING

FREDRIC MARCH
and
VERONICA LAKE

with

Robert Benchley · Susan Hayward · Cecil Kellaway

A RENE CLAIR Production · Directed by Rene Clair

Screen Play by Robert Pirosh and Marc Connelly
Released thru United Artists

THE PASSIONATE WITCH

Thorne Smith's raciest story is now the year's different comedy-romance!

Do You Remember?

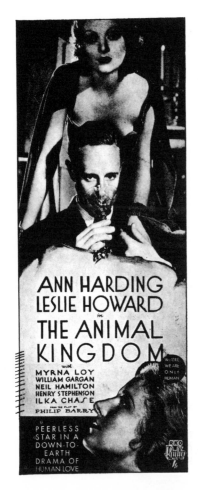

They Changed Her Tears to Laughter!

Her three goofy pals "took" the movie star she loved— but gave him back to her with everything they had!...It's love story will choke you up a little —then cheer you up plenty with its laughs and songs!

Bottoms Up

FOX PICTURE

with

**SPENCER TRACY
"PAT" PATERSON
JOHN BOLES**

Herbert Mundin • Sid Silvers
Harry Green • Thelma Todd

Produced by B. G. DeSylva
Directed by David Butler

Made by the producers of "Sunny Side Up" — and surpassing it in everything!

• For those who like to laugh and sing when tears get in their eyes!

3D

Ideal Film Pictures   Presents

Constance Binney

in

"A Bill Of Divorcement"

From Clemence Dane's Terrific Stage Hit of 1921-1922

ASSOCIATED EXHIBITORS

RKO PATHE presents

Tom KEENE

ACE OF WESTERN WHIRLWINDS

PARTNERS

FRED ALLEN

a JESSE L. LASKY production

SPRINGTIME for HENRY

OTTO **KRUGER**
NIGEL **BRUCE**
HERBERT **MUNDIN**

NANCY **CARROLL**
HEATHER **ANGEL**

from the play by
BENN W. LEVY
Directed by
FRANK TUTTLE

FOX

19

LUCKY IN LOVE

All Talking All Singing

with
MORTON DOWNEY

Story and Dialogue by Gene Markey · · Directed by
Kenneth Webb · · · · · · Supervised by Robert Kane

Pathé Picture

THE PICTURE THAT'S THE TALK OF THE NATION!

Here it is, the famous M-G-M Musical of
seven kidnapped belles, courted and kissed
right down to the shotgun wedding!

Glorious in

CINEMASCOPE

and
Blushing COLOR!

M-G-M's "SEVEN BRIDES FOR SEVEN BROTHERS"

LOVE-MAKING SONGS!

"When You're In Love"
"Bless Yore Beautiful Hide"
"Goin' Co'tin'"
"Wonderful, Wonderful Day"

...and more songs!

"Sobbin' Women"
"Spring, Spring, Spring"
"June Bride"
"Lament"

STARRING

JANE POWELL · HOWARD KEEL

with
JEFF RICHARDS · RUSS TAMBLYN · TOMMY RALL
Screen Play by
ALBERT HACKETT & FRANCES GOODRICH and DOROTHY KINGSLEY
Based On the Story "THE SOBBIN' WOMEN" by STEPHEN VINCENT BENET
Lyrics by JOHNNY MERCER · Music by GENE de PAUL · Choreography by MICHAEL KIDD
Color by   Directed by   Produced by
ANSCO · STANLEY DONEN · JACK CUMMINGS
AN M-G-M PICTURE

LESTER F. SCOTT, Jr.
presents

BUFFALO BILL, Jr.
IN

"The Ridin' Rowdy"

DIRECTED BY
RICHARD THORPE
STORY BY
WALTER J. COBURN
PRODUCED BY
ACTION PICTURES, INC.

Do You Remember?

CHARLIE CHAPLIN

"THE GOLD RUSH"

23

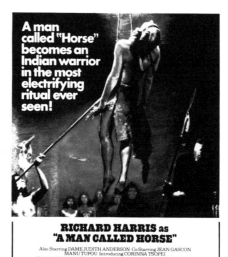

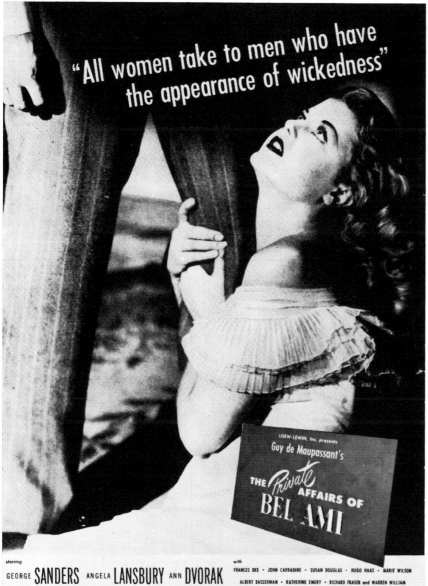

25

HAL ROACH presents
CHARLEY CHASE in "LONG FLIV THE KING!" WITH MARTHA SLEEPER

Pathécomedy

"What Price Glory" and "The Cock-Eyed World" were only dress rehearsals for

HOT PEPPER
with EDMUND LOWE
VICTOR McLAGLEN
Lupe Velez El Brendel

A comedy drama with the characters Quirt and Flagg originally created by Laurence Stallings and Maxwell Anderson.

Fox Picture   Directed by John Blystone

BUDDY ROOSEVELT in "The Ramblin' Galoot"

A Tense, Rapid-Fire Action Drama Brimful of Humor and Suspense!

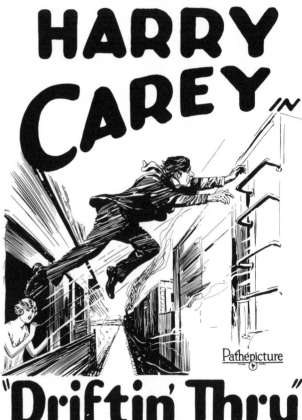

HARRY CAREY in

Pathépicture

"Driftin' Thru"
A Breath of the West—
The click of guns—the clink of glasses, the creak of leather—the murmer of mountain streams—
Riding—Fighting—Red Blood Romance
Big Chances and Big Rewards
AND A ROLLICKING COMEDY

"OUR GANG" in GOOD CHEER

"Who's nervous?
I'm SCARED STIFF!"

"Cut it out, Jerry!
You're making a
SPOOK-tacle of yourself!"

If horror pictures leave you limp,
this'll break you up with glee...
'cause when they go hauntin' haunted
castles...you'll SCREAM—with laughter!

They're even Funnier when they're

SCARED STIFF

in HAL
WALLIS'
PRODUCTION

WITH
GEORGE DOLENZ · DOROTHY MALONE
WILLIAM CHING · Directed by George Marshall
Screenplay by Herbert Baker and Walter DeLeon
Additional Dialogue by Ed Simmons and Norman Lear
Based on a play by Paul Dickey and Charles W. Goddard

 A PARAMOUNT PICTURE

SONGS!
THE BONGO BINGO
WHEN SOMEONE WONDERFUL
THINKS YOU'RE WONDERFUL
THE ENCHILADA MAN
WHAT HAVE YOU DONE FOR ME LATELY
I DON'T CARE IF THE SUN DON'T SHINE
YOU HIT THE SPOT
MAMAE EU QUERO

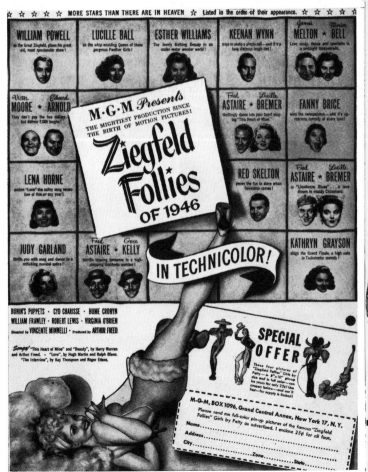

29

Critics' Quotes

Critics' quotes are frequently used in ads to sell all types of movies, although foreign films rely on them more. Usually the ads attempt to illustrate a film's favorable reception by featuring numerous excerpts. But the use of a single laudatory review in its complete form, if the critic is considered particularly influential and the review is so outstanding, is not uncommon.

In the '40's, a studio lauded the critic's role in the industry. Warner Brothers used this ploy to subtly compliment itself. Most of the ad for *In Our Time* concerned the awards and acclamations given to Warner Brothers pictures in 1943.

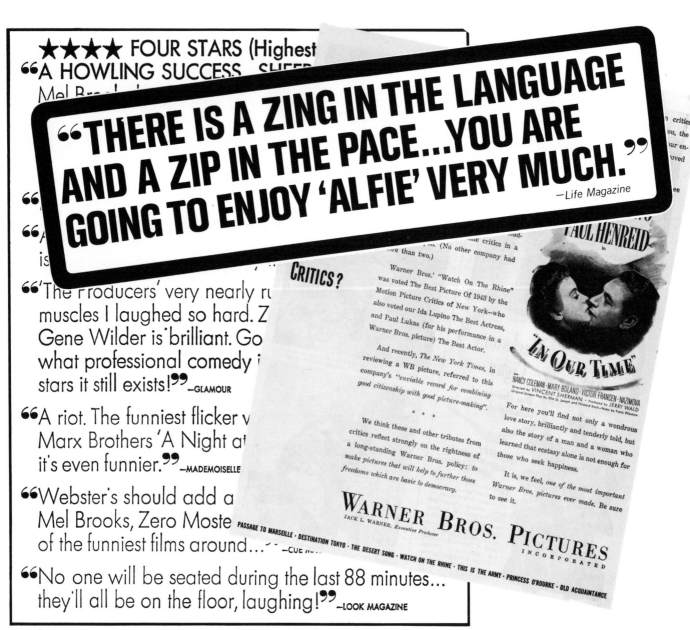

★★★★ FOUR STARS (Highest
"A HOWLING SUCCESS...SHEER
Mel Brooks...

"THERE IS A ZING IN THE LANGUAGE AND A ZIP IN THE PACE...YOU ARE GOING TO ENJOY 'ALFIE' VERY MUCH."
—Life Magazine

"'The Producers' very nearly ru
muscles I laughed so hard. Z
Gene Wilder is brilliant. Go
what professional comedy i
stars it still exists!" —GLAMOUR

"A riot. The funniest flicker v
Marx Brothers 'A Night at
it's even funnier." —MADEMOISELLE

"Webster's should add a
Mel Brooks, Zero Moste
of the funniest films around..." —CUE N...

"No one will be seated during the last 88 minutes... they'll all be on the floor, laughing!" —LOOK MAGAZINE

CRITICS?

...e critics in a ...re than two.) (No other company had
Warner Bros.' "Watch On The Rhine" was voted The Best Picture Of 1943 by the Motion Picture Critics of New York—who also voted our Ida Lupino The Best Actress, and Paul Lukas (for his performance in a Warner Bros. picture) The Best Actor.

And recently, *The New York Times*, in reviewing a WB picture, referred to this company's "*enviable record for combining good citizenship with good picture-making*".

* * *

We think these and other tributes from critics reflect strongly on the rightness of a long-standing Warner Bros. policy: to make pictures that will help to further those freedoms which are basic to democracy.

PAUL HENREID
in
"IN OUR TIME"
NANCY COLEMAN · MARY BOLAND · VICTOR FRANCEN · NAZIMOVA
Directed by VINCENT SHERMAN · Produced by JERRY WALD
Original Screen Play by Ellis St. Joseph and Howard Koch · Music by Franz Waxman

For here you'll find not only a wondrous love story, brilliantly and tenderly told, but also the story of a man and a woman who learned that ecstasy alone is not enough for those who seek happiness.

It is, we feel, one of the most important Warner Bros. pictures ever made. Be sure to see it.

WARNER BROS. PICTURES
JACK L. WARNER, *Executive Producer*
INCORPORATED

PASSAGE TO MARSEILLE · DESTINATION TOKYO · THE DESERT SONG · WATCH ON THE RHINE · THIS IS THE ARMY · PRINCESS O'ROURKE · OLD ACQUAINTANCE

Gimmee the Schmeer

One of the more colorful terms which is widely used in movie advertising is *schmeer*. A schmeer campaign, as might be deduced from its very sound, does not refer to a classic "white space" approach. When a producer says "Gimme a schmeer!" he wants an ad which can only be described as busy.

Generally, every inch of schmeer space is filled with illustrations of action scenes from the film and a voluminous amount of descriptive copy (SEE! SEE! SEE!) acclaiming the extraordinary and spectacular qualities of the film (A CAST OF THOUSANDS... TECHNICOLOR...WIDESCREEN...YEARS IN THE MAKING!).

A schmeer is usually substituted for a "class" ad when a film ends its limited engagement run at a prestigious big city theatre and/or intimate art theatre and is released for general distribution at the neighborhood theatres (better known as the "nabes"). The two different ads for *The Ten Commandments* are typical examples of this practice.

Although biblical movies, epics, lavish musicals and westerns lend themselves to a schmeer campaign, this approach is often employed for other types of films as well. It is hoped that by employing the schmeer approach, films which would appeal to only a specialized audience will attract a wider segment of the movie public. Schmeer

ads for serious dramas like *Viva Zapata* (1952) and George Bernard Shaw's talky *Caesar and Cleopatra* (1946) exemplify this sales strategy. With *Zapata* they were attempting to reach the action audience, selling a psychological drama as an action-packed western. *Caesar and Cleopatra*'s ads were aimed at the spectacle-oriented audience.

Gimmee the Schmeer

Note pre-schmeer and schmeer ads
for *The Greatest Story Ever Told.*

UNPRECEDENTED SCENES OF SWEEP AND SPLENDOR RE-STAGE THE BUILDING OF THE FIRST WONDER OF THE WORLD——THE GREAT PYRAMID AT GIZA!

THOUSANDS OF ACTORS AND EXTRAS!	16 CINEMASCOPE COLOR-CAMERAS!	21,000 WORKERS AND TECHNICIANS!	1600 CAMELS! 104 SPECIALLY BUILT BARGES!

3 YEARS IN RESEARCH! 9,753 PLAYERS IN ONE SCENE ALONE!

FILMED IN EGYPT BY THE LARGEST LOCATION CREW EVER SENT ABROAD FROM HOLLYWOOD!	ITS MUSIC BY ACADEMY AWARD WINNER, DIMITRI TIOMKIN!	ITS STORY FROM THE NOBEL PRIZE AND PULITZER PRIZE PEN OF WILLIAM FAULKNER!

Warner Bros. PRESENT

HOWARD HAWKS' **LAND OF THE PHARAOHS**

WARNERCOLOR · CINEMASCOPE · STEREOPHONIC SOUND

STARRING **JACK HAWKINS** · **JOAN COLLINS** · **DEWEY MARTIN** · **ALEXIS MINOTIS**

Written by William Faulkner · Harry Kurnitz · Harold Jack Bloom

Produced and Directed by HOWARD HAWKS · Presented by WARNER BROS.

Music Composed and Conducted by Academy Award Winner DIMITRI TIOMKIN

Her treachery stained every stone of the Pyramid!

"I bought this woman for my own... and I'll kill the man who touches her!"

They live again... the fearless men and women whose daring drew the map of America across the wilderness... in lines of their own blood!

GARY COOPER · PAULETTE GODDARD
in Cecil B. DeMille's
UNCONQUERED
Color by TECHNICOLOR
with
HOWARD DA SILVA · BORIS KARLOFF · CECIL KELLAWAY · WARD BOND

Primitive Love! Romance flames on civilization's last frontier... where there was only one law that had to be obeyed!

Slave Auction! Where a villain could buy a murderer... or a lonely man could bargain for a wife!

Produced and Directed by Cecil B. DeMille
Screenplay by Charles Bennett, Fredric M. Frank and Jesse Lasky, Jr
Based on the novel by Neil H. Swanson
A PARAMOUNT PICTURE

LIFE "THE MOST COLOSSAL EVER!" Look
MGM
QUO VADIS
in TECHNICOLOR

ROBERT TAYLOR · DEBORAH KERR
LEO GENN · PETER USTINOV
JOHN LEE MAHIN · S. N. BEHRMAN · SONYA LEVIEN
MERVYN LeROY · SAM ZIMBALIST

TWO YEARS IN THE MAKING!   A FORTUNE TO PRODUCE!

M-G-M's Magnificent CinemaScope and COLOR Spectacle!

"THE PRODIGAL"

The story of Woman's Beauty and Man's Temptation!

UNFORGETTABLE THRILLS!
• Destruction of the love temple of the pagan gods!
• Beautiful maidens on the human wheel of fortune!
• Amazing rites of the pagan love goddess Astarte!
• Revolt of the dungeon slaves in sinful Damascus!
• The Garden of Love where The Prodigal meets the pagan beauty!
• The scarlet wall of a shameless city!
• The battle in the vulture pit!
CAST OF THOUSANDS IN THESE AND MANY OTHER PULSE-POUNDING SPECTACLES!

LANA TURNER · EDMUND PURDOM · LOUIS CALHERN   with AUDREY DALTON · JAMES MITCHELL
NEVILLE BRAND · WALTER HAMPDEN · TAINA ELG · FRANCIS L. SULLIVAN · JOSEPH WISEMAN · SANDRA DESCHER screen play MAURICE ZIMM directed by RICHARD THORPE produced by CHARLES SCHNEE

37

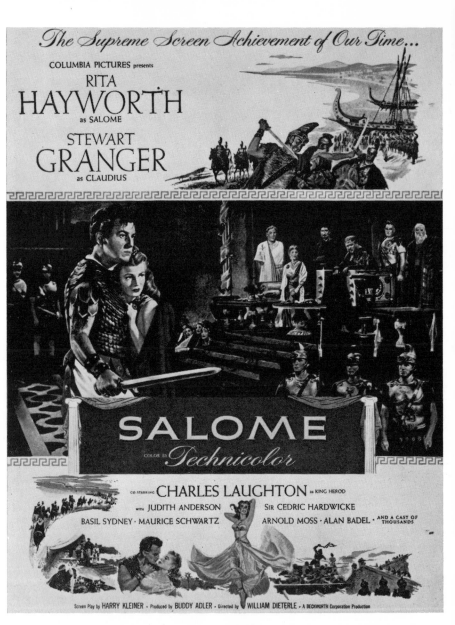

It's Here!
The thundering story that
challenges all filmdom to
match its excitement!
*"Iron Rails to Kansas . . .
Iron Nerves from there on!"*

WARNER BROS. PRESENT

ERROL FLYNN
OLIVIA DeHAVILLAND
in
Santa Fe Trail
A thousand miles of danger with a thousand thrills a mile!

Original Screen Play
by Robert Buckner
Music by Max Steiner

with RAYMOND MASSEY
RONALD REAGAN • ALAN HALE
Wm. Lundigan • Van Heflin • Gene Reynolds
Henry O'Neill • Guinn 'Big Boy' Williams
DIRECTED BY MICHAEL CURTIZ

WATCH!
The big hit right after
'Santa Fe Trail' will be
'FOUR MOTHERS!'
It's the wonderful new
Warner Bros. picture
starring the 'Four
Daughters'!

41

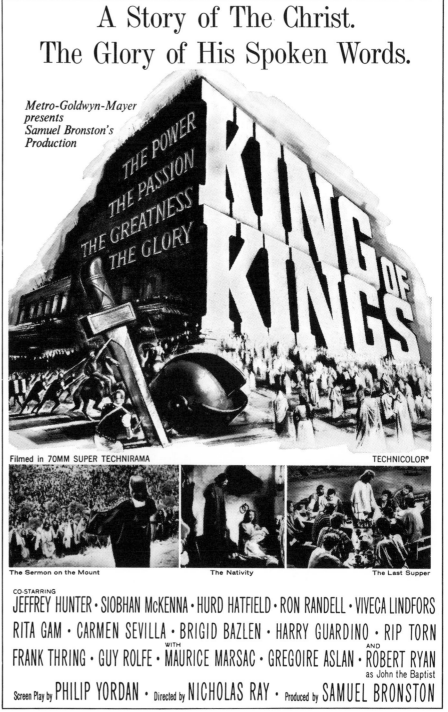

Logos

Down Madison Ave

"PUTNEY SWOPE"

The Truth and Soul Movie

A logo is the figurative representation of a film's meaning, its title, its plot, and so forth, as differentiated from photographs, portraits, etc., that tend to be more literal in their execution. A successful logo becomes a symbol of the film for which it is used and becomes readily identifiable as its trademark.

Logos serve a practical purpose as well as being attention-getting. In an era of cost-cutting on the part of the studios and other moviemakers, the logo can be used effectively in small ads, thus reducing advertising expenditures.

Saul Bass, who has designed the logos for the majority of Otto Preminger's films, is considered the ackowledged master of this art form. His logo for *The Man with the Golden Arm* won worldwide recognition. Although this was not his first logo (*Carmen Jones* preceded it), it is considered the forerunner of the technique.

Some movies seem to demand the use of a logo, *Z* being a good example.

Although the ads for some movies featured artwork which became closely associated with the movie in the public's mind, there is a clear distinction between major art and logos. The ads for *Hello, Dolly!*, *Thoroughly Modern Millie* and *The Sound of Music* and the famous Norman Rockwell painting for *The Song of Bernadette* feature major art, while *Anatomy of a Murder*, *Putney Swope* and *Advise and Consent* utilize the logo.

THE SENSATIONAL HIT THAT'S RAISING THE ROOF

Are the men and women in Washington really like this?

The Nominee

The Foe

The Blackmailed

The Leader

The Playboy

The Hostess

The President

The V.P.

The Informer   The Blackmailer   The Wife

"What happened in Hawaii? That awful creature on the phone made it sound like he knew some kind of a nasty secret!"

Thomas Wiseman— Sunday Express

EXCELLENT

ADVISE & CONSENT

CERT X ADULTS ONLY

OTTO PREMINGER PRESENTS HENRY FONDA ☆ CHARLES LAUGHTON ☆ DON MURRAY WALTER PIDGEON ☆ PETER LAWFORD ☆ GENE TIERNEY ☆ FRANCHOT TONE ☆ LEW AYRES BURGESS MEREDITH ☆ EDDIE HODGES ☆ PAUL FORD ☆ GEORGE GRIZZARD ☆ INGA SWENSON

WITH PAUL McGRATH, EDWARD ANDREWS, WILL GEER, BETTY WHITE, TOM HELMORE, HILLARY EAVES, RENE PAUL, MICHELE MONTAU, PAUL STEVENS, RUSS BROWN, MALCOLM ATTERBURY, SCREENPLAY BY WENDELL MAYES, BASED ON THE NOVEL BY ALLEN DRURY, MUSIC BY JERRY FIELDING, PHOTOGRAPHED IN PANAVISION ® BY SAM LEAVITT, PRODUCTION DESIGNED BY LYLE WHEELER, A COLUMBIA PICTURES RELEASE THROUGH B.L.C. PRODUCED AND DIRECTED BY OTTO PREMINGER

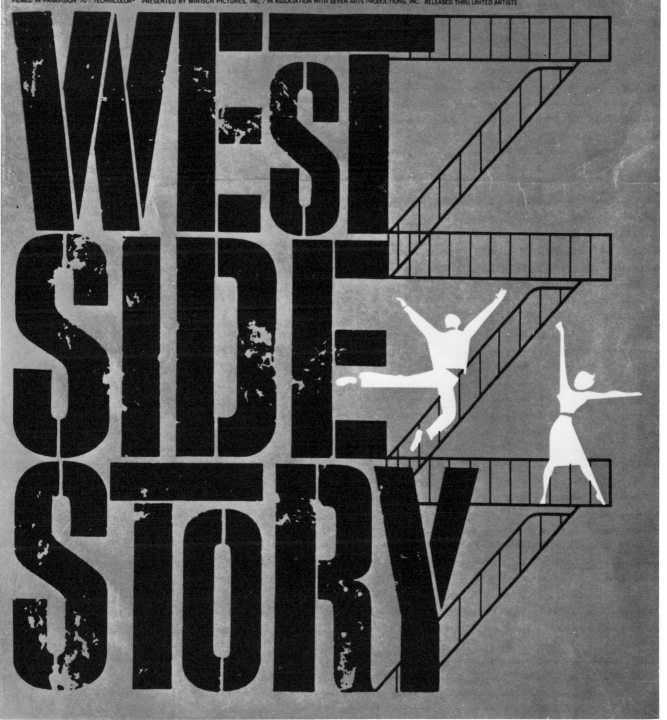

MIRISCH PICTURES PRESENTS "WEST SIDE STORY" A ROBERT WISE PRODUCTION STARRING NATALIE WOOD

RICHARD BEYMER   RUSS TAMBLYN   RITA MORENO   GEORGE CHAKIRIS

DIRECTED BY ROBERT WISE AND JEROME ROBBINS SCREENPLAY BY ERNEST LEHMAN ASSOCIATE PRODUCER SAUL CHAPLIN
CHOREOGRAPHY BY JEROME ROBBINS MUSIC BY LEONARD BERNSTEIN LYRICS BY STEPHEN SONDHEIM
BASED UPON THE STAGE PLAY PRODUCED BY ROBERT E. GRIFFITH AND HAROLD S. PRINCE
BOOK BY ARTHUR LAURENTS PLAY CONCEIVED, DIRECTED AND CHOREOGRAPHED BY JEROME ROBBINS PRODUCTION DESIGNED BY BORIS LEVEN / MUSIC CONDUCTED BY JOHNNY GREEN
FILMED IN PANAVISION* 70 / TECHNICOLOR*   PRESENTED BY MIRISCH PICTURES, INC. / IN ASSOCIATION WITH SEVEN ARTS PRODUCTIONS, INC.   RELEASED THRU UNITED ARTISTS

WEST SIDE STORY

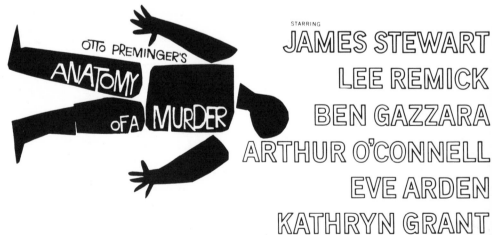

FILMING
COMPLETED TODAY!

PALOMAR PICTURES INTERNATIONAL PRESENTS
AN ASSOCIATES AND ALDRICH PRODUCTION "The
Killing
of Sister
George"

THE KILLING OF SISTER GEORGE
STARRING BERYL REID · SUSANNAH YORK · CORAL BROWNE
ALSO STARRING RONALD FRASER · PATRICIA MEDINA
HUGH PADDICK · MURRAY MATHESON
FROM THE PLAY BY FRANK MARCUS · SCREENPLAY BY LUKAS HELLER
PRODUCED AND DIRECTED BY ROBERT ALDRICH
FROM CINERAMA RELEASING CORPORATION · COLOR

"THE DRAMA AND THE PASSION OF
ONE OF THE EPIC EVENTS OF THE
TWENTIETH CENTURY!"
LIFE MAGAZINE

OTTO PREMINGER PRESENTS
PAUL NEWMAN / EVA MARIE SAINT
RALPH RICHARDSON / PETER LAWFORD
LEE J. COBB / SAL MINEO / JOHN DEREK
JILL HAWORTH

SCREENPLAY BY DALTON TRUMBO / BASED ON THE NOVEL BY LEON URIS / MUSIC BY ERNEST GOLD / PHOTOGRAPHED IN SUPER PANAVISION
TECHNICOLOR® BY SAM LEAVITT / A UNITED ARTISTS RELEASE / PRODUCED AND DIRECTED BY OTTO PREMINGER ·

Here is greatness...
wonder...majesty
...a motion picture no
human words can
describe...but which
every human heart can
feel...and share.

Franz Werfel's
THE SONG OF BERNADETTE
with
JENNIFER JONES • WILLIAM EYTHE
CHARLES BICKFORD • VINCENT
PRICE • LEE J. COBB

Directed by HENRY KING • Produced by WILLIAM PERLBERG • Screen Play by George Seaton • A **20**TH CENTURY-FOX PICTURE

YVES MONTAND   IRENE PAPAS   JEAN-LOUIS TRINTIGNANT

rected by Costa-Gavras   Screenplay by Jorge Semprun   Music by Mikis Theodorakis   From the Novel *Z*
by Vassili Vassilikos   In Eastmancolor

SANDY DENNIS · KEIR DULLEA · ANNE HEYWOOD
AS ELLEN MARCH

D. H. LAWRENCE'S
THE FOX

...*symbol of the male*..

Movies from Other Media

Almost from the beginning, filmmakers recognized the merits of using other media as sources for their movies. Through the years films have been adapted from such varied areas as novels, radio programs, comic strips, plays and television shows. Several factors contribute to the movie industry's reliance on external creative ideas. After the public became bored with the novelty of motion pictures, they demanded more complex plots and the relatively high cost of making a film necessitated choosing a proven property.

There is a great advantage for the ad man when a film is adapted from a "hit" in another medium. The initial hurdle of introducing the movie to the public is made easier, as they are already familiar with the characters and the story line. The popularity of a hit play or best-selling book can easily be exploited in films. And, of course, exhibitors are more eager to book a film that seems to have built-in audience appeal.

An average best-selling novel in its hardback edition may only have been read by 100,000 people. Perhaps an additional half million readers got to it in paperback, magazine and newspaper serializations. But what the film company has bought in addition to the property is the vast amount of publicity and advertising the book has received. Though people may not have read it personally, they know about it, and many are waiting for the film version.

When a film which originated in another medium is released, the advertising naturally plays up this fact. But the degree to which the method is employed often varies from film to film. In posters for *The Good Earth,* for example, the book is emphasized with a picture of the novel shown to remind the potential moviegoer that the film version has finally arrived. *The Good Earth* had become almost a classic by 1937 and the quiet tone of the campaign reflected the studio's awareness of this.

Along with the popularity of the book *A Tree Grows in Brooklyn,* the advertising campaign for the film in 1945 exploited the movie's ability to bring to life the characters presented on the printed page. The ads showed paintings of the actors who were portraying the various characters. By personalizing the characters of Betty Smith's book and conveying the message that the audience could see them on screen, the ads gave a new dimension to the movie version of a widely read novel.

The advertising for the film *Lolita* shrewdly capitalized on the sensational nature of that book, with a terrific, thought-provoking copy line: "How did they ever make a film of *Lolita*?" It accomplished several objectives. The copy line itself was an eye- and ear-catcher. Its underlying message combatted one of the few problems faced by a movie adapted from a famous book. It reached the book-oriented segment of the population that shuns movie versions of its favorite novels, the people with the line "No, I'm not going to see how they've ruined the story, I've read the book." Even this group was intrigued by *Lolita*'s inventive ad line.

*Judgment at Nuremberg
was first a successful TV Special.*

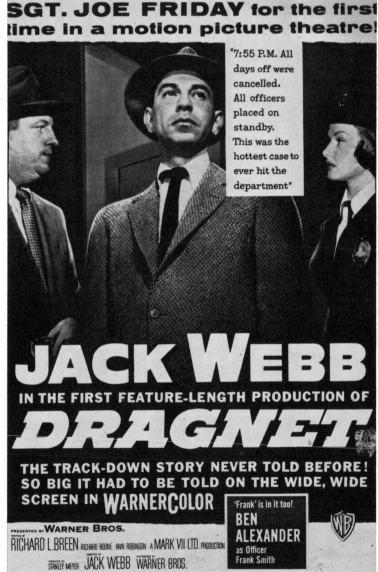

The
WILLIAM WYLER
RAY STARK
Production

COLUMBIA PICTURES and RASTAR PRODUCTIONS present

BARBRA STREISAND · OMAR SHARIF in "FUNNY GIRL"

co-starring
KAY MEDFORD · ANNE FRANCIS · WALTER PIDGEON as Florenz Ziegfeld
Musical Numbers Directed by HERBERT ROSS · Music by JULE STYNE · Lyrics by BOB MERRILL
Based on the Musical Play by ISOBEL LENNART · Music by JULE STYNE · Lyrics by BOB MERRILL
Screenplay by ISOBEL LENNART · Produced by RAY STARK · Directed by WILLIAM WYLER
Production Designed by GENE CALLAHAN · Musical Supervision WALTER SCHARF · Miss Streisand's Costumes by IRENE SHARAFF
TECHNICOLOR® · PANAVISION® · Original Soundtrack Album on Columbia Records

Academy
Award
Winner
**BEST
ACTRESS**
Barbra
Streisand

Suggested for
GENERAL audiences.

NORTH AFRICA...   SALERNO...ANZIO...VOLTURNO...
HE WAS THERE!

The exciting true-life story
of America's most decorated
hero... AUDIE MURPHY!

TO HELL AND BACK

CinemaScope   From the best-selling autobiography   PRINT BY **TECHNICOLOR**

A Universal-International Picture starring **AUDIE MURPHY** with MARSHALL THOMPSON · CHARLES DRAKE · GREGG PALMER · JACK KELLY · PAUL PICERNI · SUSAN KOHNER
Directed by JESSE HIBBS · Written for the Screen by GIL DOUD · Produced by AARON ROSENBERG

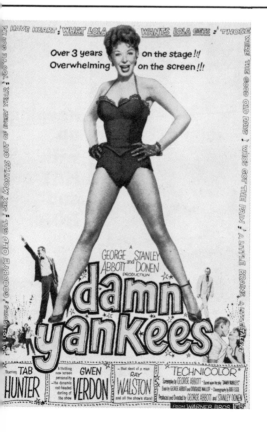
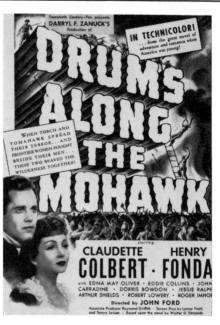

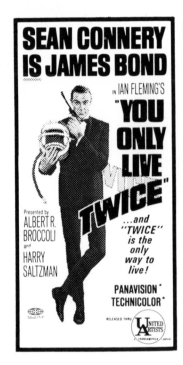

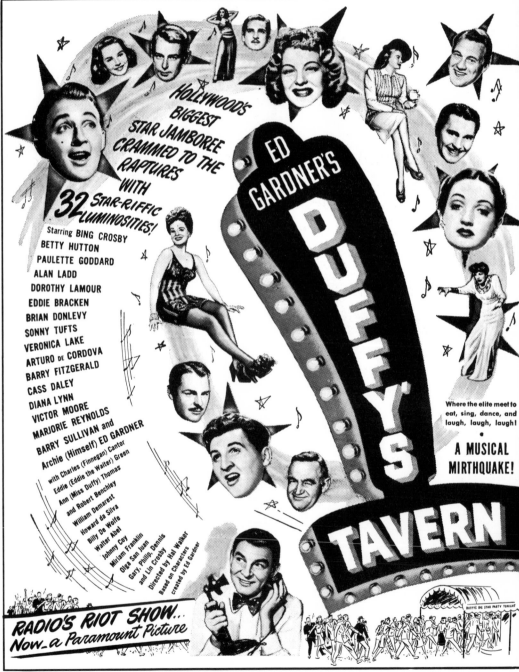

This is the year of "The Yearling"

Love conquers a wilderness! · A feud flares into violence! · Peck's finest performance! · It's kill the bear... or starve! · A great book comes to life!

M.G.M. presents in Technicolor
THE YEARLING

starring GREGORY PECK · JANE WYMAN · A CLARENCE BROWN PRODUCTION · CLAUDE JARMAN, JR. as "Jody"

· Bevans · Margaret Wycherly · Forrest Tucker · Screen Play by Paul Osborn · Based on the Pulitzer Prize Novel by Marjorie Kinnan Rawlings · Directed by Clarence Brown · Produced by SIDNEY FRANKLIN · A Metro-Goldwyn-Mayer Picture

WHAT ABOUT TRADER HORN?
WHAT ABOUT TRADER HORN?
WHAT ABOUT TRADER HORN?
The world has been waiting impatiently while METRO-GOLDWYN-MAYER has been pouring men, money and genius into the creation of its greatest motion picture! AT LAST—

TRADER HORN

FILMED IN THE WILDS OF AFRICA
Based on the famous novel by TRADER HORN & ETHELREDA LEWIS
Directed by W. S. VAN DYKE
with HARRY CAREY · DUNCAN RENALDO · EDWINA BOOTH

is completed and has been proclaimed greater than "THE BIG PARADE" greater than "BEN HUR," in fact
"THE GREATEST ADVENTURE PICTURE OF ALL TIME!"
See it at your favorite theatre

A METRO GOLDWYN MAYER

A Fiery Girl Who Dares The Dangers Of The Sea And A Savage Land... Fighting For The 'Love Of A Bold Adventurer!

M-G-M presents
GREEN DOLPHIN STREET

M-G-M'S $275,000 PRIZE NOVEL IS ON THE SCREEN!

Lana Turner

VAN HEFLIN · DONNA REED · RICHARD HART
FRANK MORGAN · EDMUND GWENN · DAME MAY WHITTY · REGINALD OWEN · GLADYS COOPER
DIRECTED BY VICTOR SAVILLE · PRODUCED BY CAREY WILSON

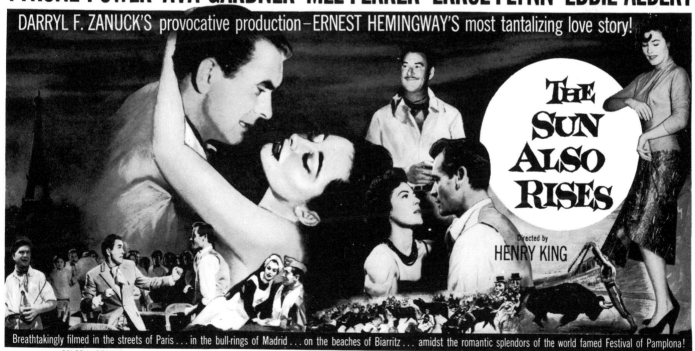

20th Century-Fox presents the love story that was too daring to film until now...with the cast that took two years to assemble!

TYRONE POWER · AVA GARDNER · MEL FERRER · ERROL FLYNN · EDDIE ALBERT

DARRYL F. ZANUCK'S provocative production—ERNEST HEMINGWAY'S most tantalizing love story!

THE SUN ALSO RISES

Directed by
HENRY KING

Breathtakingly filmed in the streets of Paris . . . in the bull-rings of Madrid . . . on the beaches of Biarritz . . . amidst the romantic splendors of the world famed Festival of Pamplona!

COLOR by DE LUXE

CinemaScope
In the wonder of STEREOPHONIC SOUND

Featuring GREGORY RATOFF · JULIETTE GRECO · MARCEL DALIO · ROBERT EVANS   Produced by DARRYL F. ZANUCK · Screenplay by PETER VIERTEL

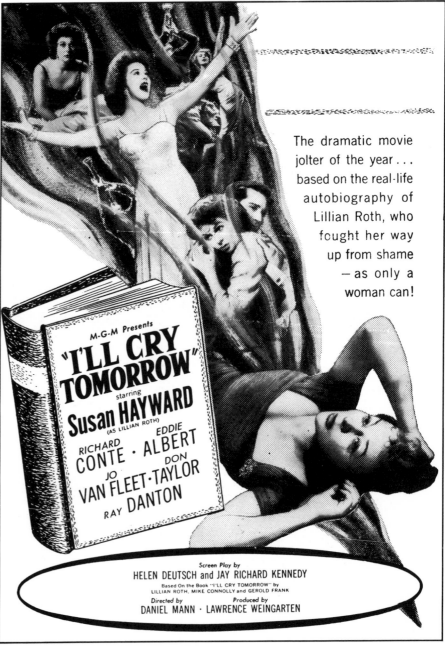

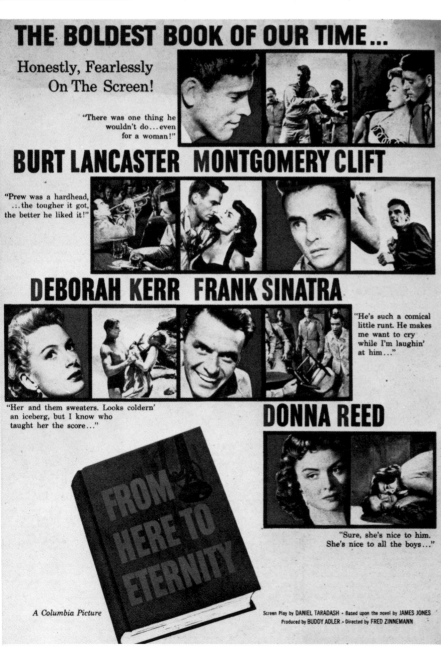

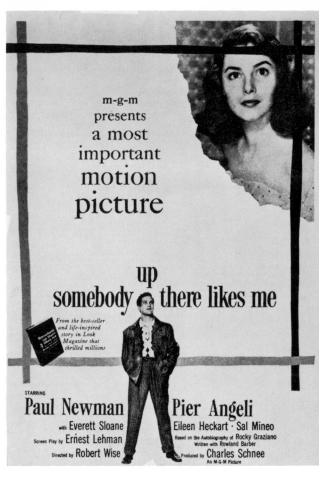

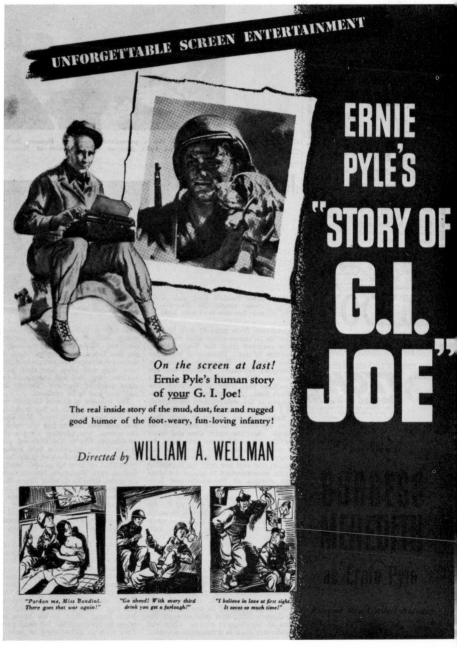

"AUNTIE MAME"

STARRING
ROSALIND
RUSSELL
ON THE SCREEN !

FILMED IN TECHNIRAMA COLOR BY TECHNICOLOR

FORREST TUCKER · CORAL BROWNE · FRED CLARK From the novel "Auntie Mame" by PATRICK DENNIS Screenplay by BETTY COMDEN and ADOLPH GREEN Directed by MORTON DaCOSTA From WARNER BROS.

UP YOUR STREET...

...a woman unfaithful

...tongues wagging neighbors pointing

...a girl...she knows her mother is wronging her father yet defends her...for she understands

This happens on any day UP YOUR STREET... on any Street... in any city ...

SAMUEL GOLDWYN presents

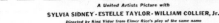

STREET SCENE

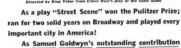

A United Artists Picture with
SYLVIA SIDNEY · ESTELLE TAYLOR · WILLIAM COLLIER, Jr.
Directed by King Vidor from Elmer Rice's play of the same name

As a play "Street Scene" won the Pulitzer Prize; ran for two solid years on Broadway and played every important city in America!

As Samuel Goldwyn's outstanding contribution to the screen it is even greater than the stage play, combining as it does all the terrific heart appeal of his success "Stella Dallas", with the dramatic sweep of King Vidor's "Big Parade".

It's on the screen so
ROAR AMERICA !

BETTE DAVIS
ANN SHERIDAN
MONTY (The Beard) WOOLLEY

"The Man Who Came to Dinner"

NOTHING COULD BE FUNNIER!

WARNER BROS. Newest Hit! With
JIMMY DURANTE · RICHARD TRAVIS
BILLIE BURKE · REGINALD GARDINER
Directed by WILLIAM KEIGHLEY
Screen Play by Julius J. & Philip G. Epstein
From the 3-year-run stage success by
GEO. S. KAUFMAN and MOSS HART
Produced by Sam H. Harris

Your theatre manager will tell you the opening date... that's your night to howl!

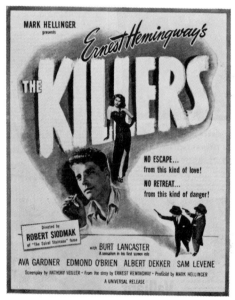

WARNER BROS. PRESENTS ALL THE HEART AND HAPPINESS OF THE BROADWAY HIT...

...THE GIRL WHO BECAME THE GREATEST SHOW IN SHOW BUSINESS.

ROSALIND RUSSELL · NATALIE WOOD · KARL MALDEN

as GYPSY ROSE LEE

GYPSY

A MERVYN LeROY PRODUCTION Based upon the play "Gypsy." Book by Arthur Laurents · Music by Jule Styne · Lyrics by Stephen Sondheim · Screenplay by Leonard Spigelgass
Directed and Choreographed by Jerome Robbins · Based upon the Memoirs of Gypsy Rose Lee · Directed by Mervyn LeRoy · TECHNICOLOR® · TECHNIRAMA® · Presented by WARNER BROS.

Comic Strip Features

One interesting method of selling a film was to present quasi-comic strip features of the story and run them as ads in national magazines. This type of ad was used as an attention-getting device to appeal to those who would normally flip by the conventional movie ads.

The comic strip approach had several things going for it. The ads often ran in full color. Newspaper comic strips and comic books were at the height of their popularity. Thus the film industry was astute enough to exploit another medium's success.

Comic strip ads personalized the characters for the potential moviegoer and hopefully told him enough of the story to intrigue him into buying a ticket. The panel format lent itself to the suspense build-up with the last panel ending (as all continuing comic strips do) leaving the reader with a thirst for more.

Naturally, when comic books and strips fell from favor in the 1950's, the industry ceased using this type of ad. But they were fun while they lasted.

One of the truly memorable features of movie advertising is
the terrific copy lines which have been created to sell various movies
and stars. Ad men agree that probably the most famous copy line
of all is "Gable's Back and Garson's Got Him!", created in 1945
for Clark Gable's return to moviemaking after service in W.W. II
(in a potboiler called *Adventure* co-starring Greer Garson). The
movie was soon forgotten but the ad line still lives.

 It was certainly not the first time that stars' names had been used
in such catchy fashion. There were many others—"*T-N-T . . .
Turner 'n Taylor . . .* They're Dynamite Together in *Johnny Eager*"
—"*Cagney* Meets a *Raft* of Trouble in *Each Dawn I Die*"—
there are hundreds more. But "Gable's Back and Garson's Got Him!"

CLARK GABLE • GREER GARSON in Victor Fleming's production of "ADVENTURE" with Joan Blondell • Thomas Mitchell
TOM TULLY • JOHN QUALEN • RICHARD HAYDN • LINA ROMAY • HARRY DAVENPORT • Screen Play by FREDERICK HAZLITT BRENNAN and VINCENT LAWRENCE • Adaptation by
Anthony Veiller and William H Wright • Based on a Novel by Clyde Brion Davis • DIRECTED BY VICTOR FLEMING • PRODUCED BY SAM ZIMBALIST • A METRO-GOLDWYN-MAYER PICTURE

caught on as no line had before it and began a new era in movie advertising ad lines.

Catchy ad lines are important because if the line catches on and is repeated and talked about, the film garners a million dollars' worth of free publicity. Two recent examples: "Love Means Never Having To Say You're Sorry" (from *Love Story*) and "Pray For Rosemary's Baby" (from *Rosemary's Baby*). These were picked up by comedians and satirists and parodied so often that the films literally became household words.

If an ad line proved to be a big success, a rival company, or the originating company, was not averse to using a variation of it. The Gable line was copied often (Garbo's Back!, etc.). The great line "Nobody's As Good As Bette When She's Bad," created for Bette Davis' 1949 disaster, *Beyond the Forest*, was imitated six years later for a Joan Crawford vehicle, *Queen Bee*. The ad line for that one was:

She's So Excitingly Good When She's So Wonderfully Bad."

Beyond the Forest had not one but two fun ad lines. In addition to "Nobody's As Good...," Bette was also billed as: "A Twelve O'Clock Girl In A Nine O'Clock Town." A fantastically successful ad line, created in 1966, was: "The Birds Is Coming," for Alfred Hitchcock's film, *The Birds*. The line was seemingly ungrammatical and was repeated everywhere. Hitchcock himself is credited with this ad line.

On the following pages are some other ads with famous tag lines. Some are great—others funny—most all are memorable.

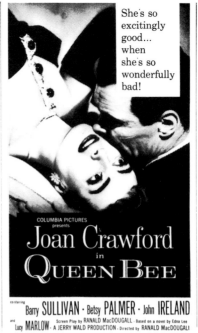

TAYLOR 'N' TURNER

"You're cruel, Johnnie. You're almost 100% bad. But whatever you are, darling, you're my man!

They're dynamite in

JOHNNY EAGER

The flaming drama of a high-born beauty who blindly loved the most icy-hearted Big Shot gangland ever knew.

A MERVYN LeROY Production with

EDWARD ARNOLD

VAN HEFLIN · ROBERT STERLING · PATRICIA DANE
GLENDA FARRELL · HENRY O'NEILL · DIANA LEWIS

Screen Play by John Lee Mahin and James Edward Grant
A METRO-GOLDWYN-MAYER PICTURE · Directed by MERVYN LeROY
Produced by JOHN W. CONSIDINE, Jr.

The copy line for *The Strange Love Of Martha Ivers* had the famous tag line: "Whisper Her Name." The line had its greatest impact when utilized in the radio campaign.

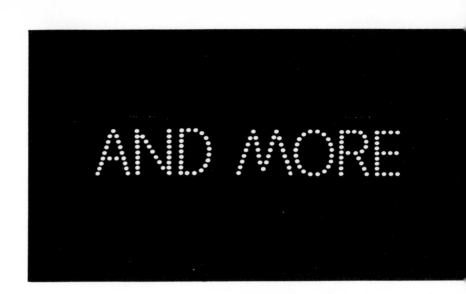

THE KIND
OF TORRID
DRAMA THAT
COMES ONLY
FROM
WARNER BROS.

private lady of a public enemy!

JOAN CRAWFORD · DAVID BRIAN
"THE DAMNED DON'T CRY!"
with STEVE COCHRAN · VINCENT SHERMAN · JERRY WALD

There NEVER was a woman like *Gilda!*

"I was true to one man once, and look what happened..."

"I didn't think I'd be true to a man again as long as I lived..."

COLUMBIA PICTURES presents
Rita HAYWORTH
as
Gilda
with
Glenn FORD
GEORGE MACREADY · JOSEPH CALLEIA
Produced by VIRGINIA VAN UPP · Directed by CHARLES VIDOR

Great as is her powerful dramatic portrayal—great, too, is this dancing Hayworth—singing "Put the Blame on Mame"!

She's got the biggest six-shooters in the west!

Betty GRABLE
as
THE *Beautiful Blonde FROM Bashful Bend*

Color by *TECHNICOLOR*

with
CESAR ROMERO · RUBY VALLEE · OLGA SAN JUAN
and STERLING HOLLOWAY · HUGH HERBERT
EL BRENDEL · PORTER HALL · PATI BEHRS
Written, Directed and Produced by
PRESTON STURGES

20th CENTURY-FOX

**NOW...
ADD
A
MOTION
PICTURE
TO
THE
WONDERS
OF
THE
WORLD!**

**TONY YUL
CURTIS BRYNNER**

in the HAROLD HECHT Production

TARAS BULBA

SAM WANAMAKER · BRAD DEXTER · GUY ROLFE · PERRY LOPEZ · George Macready · Ilka Windish · Vladimir Sokoloff

Daniel Vladimir and CHRISTINE KAUFMANN · Ocko Irman · Screenplay by WALDO SALT and KARL TUNBERG · Associate Producer Alexander Whitelaw · Music by Franz Waxman

Directed by J. LEE THOMPSON · Produced by HAROLD HECHT · Filmed in PANAVISION · EASTMANCOLOR · Released thru UNITED ARTISTS

Original Music From "TARAS BULBA"
Available on United Artists Records Album

WILL
SHE
COME
OUT
woman OR Wildcat?

Is she coming out "good", or is she coming out to avenge the terrors and the torments that make a prison for women a college for crime? This is the angry story of beautiful Marie Allen, a one-mistake girl that men betrayed ...and the law forgot!

WARNER BROS.

CAGED!

The most sensational revelations since 'Fugitive from a Chain Gang' burned into America's conscience!

WOMEN WITHOUT MEN...EXCEPT IN THEIR MEMORIES!

ELEANOR PARKER · AGNES MOOREHEAD · ELLEN CORBY · HOPE EMERSON · BETTY GARDE · JAN STERLING

PRODUCED BY JERRY WALD · WRITTEN BY VIRGINIA KELLOGG AND BERNARD C. SCHOENFELD · MUSIC BY MAX STEINER · DIRECTED BY JOHN CROMWELL

THE NEARER THEY GET TO THEIR TREASURE
THE FARTHER THEY GET FROM THE LAW!

...And the more they yearn for their women's arms, the fiercer is their lust for the gold that must be torn from those dangerous hills!

THE **TREASURE OF THE SIERRA MADRE**

WARNER BROS.
hit a new high in high adventure... bringing another great best-seller to the screen!

STARRING **HUMPHREY BOGART** AND **WALTER HUSTON** · TIM HOLT · BRUCE BENNETT

DIRECTED BY JOHN HUSTON · PRODUCED BY HENRY BLANKE

SCREEN PLAY BY JOHN HUSTON · BASED ON THE NOVEL BY B. TRAVEN · MUSIC BY MAX STEINER

94

"I WANT TO LIVE LIKE A MAN...
AND STILL BE A WOMAN!"

20th
CENTURY-FOX
presents

*Hilda
Crane*

starring

JEAN SIMMONS
GUY MADISON
JEAN PIERRE
AUMONT

with JUDITH EVELYN • EVELYN VARDEN

Print by TECHNICOLOR

CinemaScope

Produced by HERBERT B. SWOPE, JR.
Written for the Screen and Directed by PHILIP DUNNE
From the Play by Samson Raphaelson

JEAN SIMMONS gifted young star of "The Robe", "Desiree", "Guys and Dolls", achieves new dramatic stature in "Hilda Crane"— the unforgettable portrait of an unconventional woman.

THE STORY OF
RUBY GENTRY,
WHO WRECKED
A WHOLE
TOWN--

MAN BY MAN
...SIN BY
SIN!

BERNHARD-VIDOR
PRODUCTIONS, INC. presents

JENNIFER
JONES
CHARLTON
HESTON
KARL
MALDEN

"Ruby Gentry..!"

so dangerous...destructive...deadly...to love!

PRODUCED BY
JOSEPH BERNHARD & KING VIDOR
DIRECTED BY   SCREENPLAY BY
KING VIDOR • SILVIA RICHARDS

I am
TONDELAYO!

HEDY
LAMARR
Walter
PIDGEON

WHITE
CARGO

FRANK MORGAN

RICHARD CARLSON REGINALD OWEN
HENRY O'NEILL

A Metro-Goldwyn-Mayer Picture

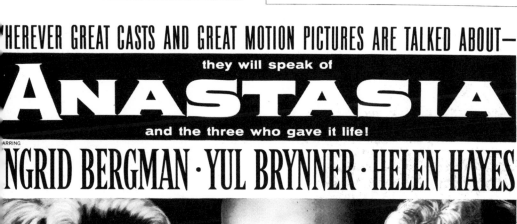

Every father's daughter is a virgin

PARAMOUNT PICTURES PRESENTS

GOODBYE, COLUMBUS

A STANLEY R. JAFFE PRODUCTION starring
RICHARD BENJAMIN JACK KLUGMAN co starring NAN MARTIN
AND INTRODUCING
ALI MacGRAW SCREENPLAY BY BASED ON THE PRODUCED BY DIRECTED BY
ARNOLD SCHULMAN NOVELLA BY STANLEY R. JAFFE LARRY PEERCE
PHILIP ROTH
NEW SONGS BY TECHNICOLOR
THE ASSOCIATION A PARAMOUNT PICTURE

THE MOTION PICTURE WITH SOMETHING TO OFFEND EVERYONE !

Metro-Goldwyn-Mayer and Filmways present
Martin Ransohoff's Production

THE Loved One

starring
ROBERT / JONATHAN
MORSE / WINTERS
ANJANETTE COMER

Dana Andrews · Milton Berle · James Coburn
John Gielgud · Tab Hunter · Margaret Leighton
Liberace · Roddy McDowall · Robert Morley
Barbara Nichols · Lionel Stander
ROD STEIGER as "Mr. Joyboy"

FROM THE MAN WHO MADE "TOM JONES"

Screenplay by Terry Southern and Christopher Isherwood
Directed by Tony Richardson
Produced by John Calley and Haskell Wexler

WARREN BEATTY
FAYE DUNAWAY

They're young...
they're in love
...and they kill people.

BONNIE AND CLYDE

CO-STARRING
MICHAEL J. POLLARD·GENE HACKMAN·ESTELLE PARSONS Written by DAVID NEWMAN and ROBERT BENTON
Music by Charles Strouse Produced by WARREN BEATTY Directed by ARTHUR PENN TECHNICOLOR® FROM WARNER BROS.-SEVEN ARTS

You are cordially invited to George and Martha's for an evening of fun and games *

ELIZABETH TAYLOR
RICHARD BURTON
IN ERNEST LEHMAN'S PRODUCTION OF EDWARD ALBEE'S
WHO'S AFRAID OF VIRGINIA WOOLF?

* IMPORTANT EXCEPTION:
NO ONE UNDER 18 WILL
BE ADMITTED UNLESS
ACCOMPANIED BY HIS PARENT.

Also starring GEORGE SEGAL · SANDY DENNIS Screenplay by Directed by
Produced on the stage by Richard Barr and Clinton Wilder · Music by Alex North ERNEST LEHMAN · MIKE NICHOLS
PRESENTED BY WARNER BROS.

Available Now! Two great Warner Bros.' albums! ① The original musical sound track. ② The complete dramatic dialogue track.

Together Again

Since silent movie days, once two stars clicked together on screen and the movie-going public displayed a tendency to identify them as a team, Hollywood capitalized on their popularity by recasting them together in other movies. The ads usually exploited this concept by using the descriptive copy line "Together Again!" or something similar.

On many occasions, advertising referred directly to prior movies in which the team had starred.

Certain teams became so identified in the public's mind that the two names became irrevocably linked. William Powell and Myrna Loy, Nelson Eddy and Jeanette MacDonald, Fred Astaire and Ginger Rogers represent the best examples of this phenomenon. Bing Crosby, Bob Hope and Dorothy Lamour represented the screen's only menage-a-trois, romping through seven *Road* pictures, often referring to each other in their individual starring films.

The team concept flourished when the studios were at their peak, as it was comparatively easy to select appropriate vehicles and assign the stars to the roles—Mickey Rooney and Judy Garland, Joan Crawford and Clark Gable, Greer Garson and Walter Pidgeon, Alan Ladd and Veronica Lake, Rita Hayworth and Glenn Ford. However, the practice declined after the studios no longer kept rosters of contract stars.

It should be noted that sometimes actors co-starred in a number of movies but still were not considered a team. George Brent and Bette Davis made nine movies together, but weren't advertised in tandem.

Together Again

102

The only major screen team that had a publicized off-screen love affair was Spencer Tracy and Katharine Hepburn. Since they were both major stars on their own before teaming for the first time in *Woman of the Year* in 1942, and continued to be successful separately throughout their careers, they hold a special place as a classic screen team.

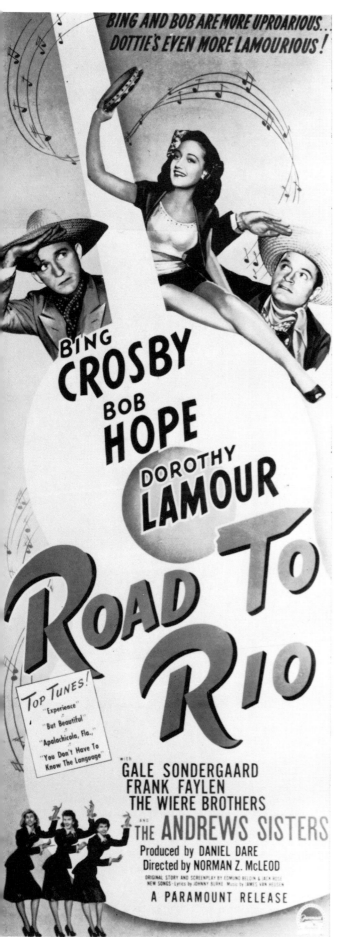

A Brief Look at Movie Advertising

Within recent years, films have been recognized as a medium worthy of the same professional criticism bestowed upon the more classical art forms. The world of movies has been explored in countless books and articles. The significance of the actor and director has been analyzed; the importance of the cameraman has been discussed; the financial plight of the industry has been exposed; and the passing of the "star system" has been mourned.

But one aspect of the business has, for the most part, escaped notice—the process through which the industry sells its product. Although little public attention has been paid to this phase of the movie business, the behind-the-scenes machinations involved in selling a movie are as fascinating, complex, creative, hectic and zany as the rest of the industry. Directors, producers, and actors have as keen an interest in the methods employed in selling the movie as in its making, for they recognized that—art form or not—an audience is still the ultimate judge of whether a film is a hit or a bomb. And deciding on the best method to attract the customers is an integral part of the business.

Moviemakers have always been aware of the importance of advertising their films. In the early days, the industry relied on fairly simple ways to solicit patrons. Handbills were distributed at strategic locations and much emphasis was placed on window cards. A primitive type of newspaper advertising was used but the new "gimmick" of moving pictures was itself such an overwhelming success with the public that intricate ads were not necessary. Most of the newspaper ads of the early days were simple announcements stating the title of the picture and, as stars emerged, the cast. Of course, as the industry mushroomed and the number of films issued each year increased, the ads reflected the increasing competition. Catchy copy lines and splashy artwork (and later photography and color) became more common.

Television and other competitive leisure time media had not yet been born in the 1920's and the motion picture industry continued to flourish. Stars were under long-term contracts and astronomical salaries were reserved for super-stars like Chaplin, Pickford, Fairbanks, and Swanson. Budgets were still relatively conservative and the huge losses absorbed by today's movie companies were unheard of. Some of the studios, in effect, acted as both distributor and exhibitor since their subsidiary companies owned huge chains of theatres. The need to sell a movie was not as compelling as it is today. Now theatre owners must be persuaded to book a picture and be convinced of its money-making potential, and the studios no longer have an assured outlet for their product. In addition, they release fewer films and each film represents a major investment. Therefore, the distributor is more concerned today than ever before with the right ad campaign.

The days of "going to the movies" as a matter of course have long since faded. Today, movie companies must vie for the public's entertainment dollar and its leisure time. The current moviegoer must be persuaded to forego his bowling game, his favorite television program, or tinkering with his stereo equipment. Movie advertising has become far more important than it ever was. The exhibitor, in most cases, is now an independent and must also be courted with a full range of blandishments to induce him to book a film.

Since control of a film's bookings no longer as easy as it was when the studios owned the theatres, huge saturation campaigns, with films opening in scores of theatres around the country, are no longer regularly feasible. Glossy full-page ads in national magazines are seldom used and the spectacular premieres designed to garner national publicity are infrequently planned. In short, the public has become more sophisticated and discriminating and the pressures on the men and women responsible for creating a successful selling campaign have escalated.

Basically, there are three ways to sell a movie—*Advertising, Publicity* and *Promotion/Exploitation.*

Paid advertising includes all news, print, radio and television spots, billboards and other areas where the distributor and/or exhibitor contracts for space.

Publicity involves obtaining "free advertising" for a film via newspaper, magazine, radio and television editorial space, feature stories, interviews, column blurbs, etc.

The terms *exploitation* and *promotion* are sometimes used interchangeably. Exploitation generally refers to exploiting a specific aspect of a movie for publicity purposes (and to generate word-of-mouth) by using gimmicks, stunts and other attention-getting devices. Promotion usually involves commercial tie-in between a film and a product and/or personality.

Advertising may be done on a national basis via TV or national magazines, in which case the distributor (the company or independent producer owning the movie) contributes one hundred percent of the total cost. Due to e difficulty in scheduling a national elease date for a movie, this type of road-based advertising (big in the 930's and '40's) is used infrequently day.

Local advertising, where the distributor and the exhibitor share the costs, now far more prevalent. Under this method, termed *cooperative advertising*, local TV and radio stations and ewspapers are utilized. Co-op advertising became necessary when exhibitors could no longer allocate the ecessary funds for what the distributor felt was an adequate campaign.

Co-op advertising usually concentrates on newspapers (rather than radio and television) because the exhibitor, since he is paying part of the campaign costs, needs the assurance that competing theatres will not benefit. For example, in a newspaper ad, only *his* theatre or group of theatres is mentioned, and he can feel confident that only *his* potential customers will see the ad. If he advertised on local radio or TV, the exhibitor would, in many cases, be giving free publicity to an exhibitor in the next town who had booked the same film. Furthermore, the costs of radio and TV advertising, even on a local basis, can be prohibitive for a small exhibitor. However, an increasing number of small independent theatre chains are developing around the country. When a chain books one film for a number of its theatres, it an justify the cost of co-op advertising n radio and TV.

Paid advertising represents the most important part of the total campaign to sell a film, and the men and women responsible for devising the ads have the most difficult job. Creating an ad for a movie is fraught with far more pitfalls than creating an ad for a new cereal or toothpaste, and the great pressure on the movie ad man results from the unique nature of the product he is selling. A motion picture is extremely perishable. Compared to toothpaste or cereal, it has a brief "shelf" life. If a picture doesn't sell within a few weeks after its release, it is, for all practical purposes, a flop. There are few second chances for a film so the first ad campaign has to be the right one.

Despite scant evidence that a new ad campaign can effect a turn-around for a film, it's a common occurrence in the industry to redesign ads and try new campaigns when the boxoffice doesn't respond.

Unlike toothpaste, which can be repackaged or reformulated, a movie cannot be reshot. It's too late to replace the stars or rewrite the script. There is only one recourse—"a new ad, and quick!" The exhibitors must be persuaded that the producer has not abandoned his picture and that a poor showing in one city does not portend disaster. It's not unusual for the producer to demand a completely new ad within 48 hours.

Another difficulty in "selling" an art form is that, by its very nature, it prohibits traditional market testing. The movie ad man, unlike his Madison Avenue counterpart, has no access to market research, tested merchandising strategies or target audience demographics. Indeed, he frequently must create an ad campaign for a film he has never seen. His sole source of inspiration may be a script which, unknown to him, has been substantially changed during shooting. If he's fortunate, he may have still photographs which were made during production. But from these scraps of information he must develop a concept which will differentiate this movie from all others ever made.

The men creating movie ads must contend not only with a lack of market research but also with problems of contractual obligations, censorship and the task of devising an overall theme which will be effective in all media.

Market Research

As has been mention previously, *market research*, which is so prevalent in other areas of advertising, is still a relatively unknown and little-used procedure in film advertising.

The movie industry has attempted to analyze the effectiveness of film titles, star names and other easily probed subjects, but the nature of the business has made any extensive attempts at market research difficult, costly and unreliable. Since a film is a curious blend of artistic and commercial ingredients, it prevents the industry from employing the more traditional forms of product testing.

A further obstacle in projecting the potential popularity of a particular film is that, unlike other consumer products, films do not really satisfy any particular need. Moreover, styles in movies usually reflect the changing mores of society and in a swiftly changing culture any attempt to anticipate the next trend is usually futile. The public is quixotic, fickle and unpredictable, as any producer who has tried to ride the crest of a trend—and failed—will tell you.

Despite all the adverse factors, some members of the movie industry are beginning to recognize that the financial risks of filmmaking have reached such proportions that a film's reception by

A Brief Look at Movie Advertising

the public cannot be left totally to chance.

In 1971, for its film *Willard*, Cinerama Distributing undertook market research, and this has become the first highly publicized case in the movie ad business. *Willard* is based on a book titled *Ratman's Notebooks* and it depicts the plight of a young man at odds with society. His entire life is a series of misfortunes, and when he establishes a relationship with a pack of rats, the film becomes a horror story, as the rats are used to dispense his own peculiar form of justice.

From the outset, Cinerama was concerned with the marketability of the subject matter. Extreme care was taken to prevent any publicity about the plot. The stars were cautioned to keep the plot from the press while on talk shows or giving newspaper interviews. But as the release date grew near, an ad campaign decision had to be made.

Cinerama had two choices—advertise the rats as the element of horror, or ignore them completely in the visual ads and copy but advertise the film as horror fare. Against their ad agency's advice, Cinerama's initial decision was to avoid any mention of rats in the ads and rely on word-of-mouth to help the picture click.

The agency—Deiner, Hauser, Greenthal (one of the top agencies in the movie ad field)—strongly favored an aggressive campaign. The dispute resulted in a decision to test market, using two Pennsylvania cities of demographic similarity, Scranton and Wilkes Barre. The ads which portrayed the rats in graphic detail were used for the Gateway Cinema in Wilkes Barre and ads with the subtler approach, which barely suggested the rat theme,

were placed for the Camerford Downtown Theatre in Scranton.

An analysis of box office receipts showed both theatres had drawn well but more thorough investigation elicited valuable information. The audience drawn by the low key (non-rat oriented) campaign consisted of all age groups but with a predominance of older people. The audience make-up in Wilkes Barre showed that the more explicit ads had attracted a predominantly youthful audience. Most were of high school age and younger. They exhibited a great deal of enthusiasm for the film and questioned when the picture would return for a regular run.

As a result of the findings, Cinerama agreed to go with the ads originally proposed by the agency. In addition, they decided to hold the film's release until school had closed to take advantage of their obvious market. And they reached the picture's natural target audience by advertising the film in school newspapers and similar publications just before schools closed.

The ads for *Willard* also contributed two memorable ad lines: "The One Movie You Should Not See Alone" and "Where Your Nightmares End...*Willard* Begins." *Willard* has proven to be a colossal hit and a sequel is planned. Whether this brief excursion into market research will be an inducement to other distributors to introduce similar techniques is difficult to judge. But, now that most of the major studios are now headed by businessmen rather than the showmen who were content to rely on their intuition, it seems inevitable that the motion picture industry will now adapt the sophisticated marketing analysis techniques perfected in other areas to its own needs.

Contractual Obligations

One of the restraints on the creativity of movie ad men is the abundance of *mandatory copy* which must appear in movie ads. The mandatory copy covers a broad spectrum of contractual obligations—the film's rating, the name of the theatre, the time schedule for viewing, etc.

Movie ad men bristled at the criticism that their ads are not as sophisticated or as clean looking as those produced by the rest of Madison Avenue. The movie ad man feels, with justification, that his effort to produce cleaner, more classic ads deserve greater recognition since it has been accomplished in spite of great obstacles.

A major contractual obligation in movie advertising concerns billing requirements. Stars, directors, screenwriters, producers, *et al.* have agreements about the use and placement of their names in ads. The regulations adopted by organizations like the Writers Guild of America must also be followed.

All billing requirements are in relation to the title of the movie and cover a broad set of circumstances. For example, a prominent star often has the right to a 70 percent or even one hundred percent billing clause written in his contract. This means that the amount of space which his name occupies in the ad must be equal to seventy percent or one hundred percent of the total amount allocated for the title of the movie. Serious disputes have erupted over violations of this clause. Stars and their agents have been known to use a ruler to measure the precise amount of space and fight over a quarter of an inch. The sequence in which a star or director's name appears is mandated by his contract or his trade organization. The determination of billing can become quite complex—for example, the size of the writer's name may vary depending on the size of the director's name. A frequent problem is that the ad man cannot take advantage of unexpected events that may occur after billing requirements have been finalized, unless contractual obligations are waived. For example, when it became apparent that Cliff Robertson had a good chance to win the Oscar for Best Actor in *Charly*, the distributor, Cinerama Releasing Corporation, wanted to launch an extensive campaign in the trade papers, as well as the general press, promoting Robertson. Contractual obligations demanded that the director and producer (in this case they were the same person, Ralph Nelson) had to be featured whenever the star's name was, and the campaign would have faltered if Nelson had not agreed to forego his "rights."

Likeness clauses are another facet to the mandatory copy problem and concern photographic and/or art representation. This area has provided the industry with several amusing anecdotes. For example, when Joseph L. Mankiewicz' production of *Cleopatra* opened in New York, the studio contracted for a giant billboard in the Times Square area to display a huge likeness of Elizabeth Taylor and Richard Burton to capitalize on all the publicity their off-screen romance had generated. The billboard was no sooner finished when Rex Harrison's agent reminded Twentieth Century-Fox of the terms of his client's contract, which stated that no likeness of Taylor or Burton could appear without his likeness also being represented in similar fashion. The new billboard had a quick visit from the painters and, within a few hours, Miss Taylor and Mr. Burton

were joined overlooking Broadway by Rex Harrison.

Censorship

The movie industry has experienced censorship, in one form or another, throughout its history. As early as the '30's the industry made an attempt at self-regulation with the establishment of the Hays Office. Every movie produced by a major studio for domestic showing was reviewed by the office before release and, if found acceptable, was awarded a seal certifying its suitability. Since there was no attempt to label films for "family viewing," "adults only," etc., all films fell into one category—general audience. There was such industry-wide agreement on the importance of self-regulation that the major studios were cooperative and complied with any suggestions concerning deletions or changes.

Although many members of the industry had minor skirmishes with the Hays office, a famous major controversy occured in 1943. The picture in question was Howard Hughes' production, *The Outlaw*, which introduced Jane Russell to the screen. The industry censors found the movie too sensational and demanded changes. Hughes, unlike his colleagues, balked at the suggestions. The dispute dragged on for a number of years and created quite a furor in the press. Eventually the seal was awarded but the film continued to be the subject of controversy as local censorship laws were invoked in many parts of the country to prevent its showing. Rather than be daunted by this type of pressure, Hughes met the situation head on, and exploited the censorship issue in the advertising for the film. The ads emphasized the

attempt to suppress *The Outlaw* and as a result Hughes turned the controversy into a selling device.

By the early 1950's, the impact of the Hays office had declined to such a degree that a major studio dared to release a film without the seal. Otto Preminger's *The Moon Is Blue* seemed to signal the end of an era when United Artists released it in defiance of the Hays office.

However, nowhere in the paid ads for *The Moon Is Blue* was it mentioned, let alone flaunted, that the film had been questioned by censors and was being released without their approval.

In retrospect, many films (Preminger's *The Man With The Golden Arm*, *Blue Denim*, *Baby Doll*), that were considered sensational by the standards of their day, would be considered relatively tame today. The advertising for these films, while titillating, only alluded to the true nature of the stories. Many of the ads adopted an implicit approach rather than the more explicit techniques used today.

The infamous ad for *Baby Doll*, showing Caroll Baker lying in a crib clothed in a slip and sucking her thumb, was considered lurid by many people. However, compared with some of the ads prevalent today, *Baby Doll* is symbolic of another age.

Eventually, the trend toward realism in movies and, therefore, movie advertising reached such proportions that the industry once again recognized that some attempt at self-regulation was required. Several factors contributed to the concern of industry magnates. Undoubtedly, the major factor was the fear that unless the industry undertook the task of policing itself, someone outside the industry (the government) might step into the breach.

A Brief Look at Movie Advertising

Although certain segments of the movie public welcomed the new freedom, there were periodic outcries on the part of Church groups and civic organizations lamenting the lack of family entertainment.

A second reason for Hollywood's move toward self regulation was the industry's concern about movie attendance. Statistics from various studios showed that weekly attendance figures had declined to approximately fifteen million from the seventy-to-ninety million averages in the late 1940's. Although there were several socio-economic factors beyond the industry's control, TV and other competing leisure-time entertainments that accounted for this decline, there was no denying that for a great number of people movies had lost their appeal.

Some people who viewed films strictly as entertainment were disappointed by realistic fare and disgusted by the trend toward sensationalism and some were parents who felt that there were few films to which they could, in good conscience, send their children.

The biggest complaint was that the industry made no attempt to label the films, and it was therefore impossible to determine the suitability of a particular movie.

Given the high cost of making a movie today, the industry knew that in order to be financially successful, a movie had to draw on a far broader section of the population than just film buffs, older teenagers, and swinging singles.

It can be safely said that the new ratings code governing films and their advertising, instituted in 1968, was not established for altruistic motives. Under the aegis of Jack Valenti, President of the Motion Picture Association of America, the industry decided to adopt a more complex and sophisticated approach to the problem.

Unlike the unsuccessful and faulty do-or-die seal concept, the new system attempted to provide guidance for the public. A series of categories was established, ranging from X—defined as a film to which children 17 or under cannot be admitted—to G, General Audiences. A review board and an appeals board composed of members of the industry were established to determine the appropriate rating for each film. Regulations were instituted concerning the manner in which the rating would be publicized in advertising and trailers. The seal, with its designated rating, had to be prominently displayed in all newspaper ads, pressbooks, TV spots, etc. Trailers for X-rated movies can only be shown during the run of G or PG films if the trailer itself is considered of G or PG calibre.

It should be noted that some theatre owners have also displayed a tendency to circumvent the new code. Instances of covering up the rating on the marquee and showing the trailer for an X-rated movie while featuring a G film have not been uncommon. Consequently, there has been widespread controversy over the effectiveness of the new code. Several church groups have withdrawn their support for the rating system, and a national magazine compared the system to other well known failures like the Edsel and Prohibition. At the present time it is rumored that the industry, under the guidance of Jack Valenti, intends to combat the criticism by instituting some reform.

Another area in which the industry has encountered censorship is far more pertinent to this discussion of movie advertising—the censorship of the ads themselves. Radio and television stations are licensed by the government, and ad men, generally speaking, know what kind of spots can be broadcast. However, for print advertising there are wide spectra, and newspapers and magazines have always demanded final approval of advertising submitted for publication.

Each newspaper and magazine serves a different potential audience and they tend to differ in their attitudes as to what constitutes an acceptable ad. One paper in town may run an ad that another paper will reject as tasteless. Normally, however, when a paper refuses an ad it gives no specific reason.

With the film *M.A.S.H.*, for example, two of the New York City dailies carried the first ad and *The New York Daily News* refused it. Art work for the print campaign was a photo of a hand giving the peace sign and supported by a pair of legs. Some papers, such as *The L.A. Times*, thought there was nudity in the art work (that the palm of the hand constituted buttocks for the legs) and insisted on a revised ad covering the area in question.

Ads for *Putney Swope* also ran into difficulty. The ads underwent substantial changes before final acceptance by most newspapers. Most of the urban newspapers and magazines accepted the art work but refused the ad line: "Up Madison Avenue." When the line was changed to "Down Madison Avenue" they ran the ad. Smaller papers and family publications often insisted on ads in which the art work was altered to delete the offensive middle finger.

Examples of arbitrary censorship by publications are numerous. Many newspapers will not carry ads which use favorable quotes from their own critics if the ad department feels the nature of the film would offend readers.

Herbert Hauser, chairman of the

board of Deiner, Hauser, Greenthal, as said that "within the recent past e have learned that censorship is on the rise."

It is a difficult task for the agency, istributor and exhibitor alike to advertise a film in a catchy, truthful nd frank manner—especially since ovie advertising must contend with egional tastes and decisions.

Radio and TV Spots

Although print remains the most opular medium for movie advertising, adio and television spot advertisements are widely used by the industry o reach specific audiences.

Care is exercised in the selection of lms to be promoted via these two edia. Radio requires that a film and ts ad campaign be conducive to strictly n audio approach. With the advent of elevision, an epic with a cast of thousands and featuring extravagant sets ill seldom be the subject of a full-cale radio campaign.

A unique and memorable copy line vhich captures the mood of the film is enerally the best approach. The line Whisper Her Name!", used for the lm, *The Secret Love of Martha Ivers*, xemplifies the type of campaign which s ideal for radio. Another considera-ion before funds are committed to a adio campaign is the designated tar-et audience. Since women and teen-gers constitute the bulk of the radio udience, a film which offered little ppeal to them would seldom be adver-ised on radio. Radio is best to remind he ticketbuyer that the film is playing t a particular theatre. The medium is ot suited for a long range pre-sell ampaign.

Television has replaced national magazines as the medium used when a picture is the subject of a national campaign, although such campaigns are infrequent today. In such a case the movie is usually a major production with lots of visual appeal. Musicals, epics, and similar spectacles are usu-ally the types of movies advertised on television. Horror films which attract children and adolescents are frequently promoted on TV during the hours when they represent the bulk of the viewers. Since TV time is so expensive, its use is usually confined to films which have broad appeal—or those with large ad budgets.

Ads are seldom broadcast during prime time because it would be too costly and not directed at the appro-priate target audience. Consequently, most ads for movies are run during the breaks of talk shows and the late-night movies since the industry feels that those audiences represent potential ticket-buyers.

Obviously ads for television are de-signed to take advantage of the me-dium's visual impact. Scenes from the movie are almost always used and crea-tive cutting techniques are employed.

Since the length of a TV or a radio spot may be one minute but is usually shorter, the ads must be exciting and dynamic to sufficiently stimulate the viewer. Unlike newspapers and maga-zines, which can be re-read at one's leisure, radio and tv spots have only one opportunity to capture the audi-ence's attention. The ad must pack a wallop in order to be memorable.

New "Art Film" Movement

Movie advertising received a shot of creative adrenalin with the huge com-mercial success of foreign films, be-ginning in the early 1950's. Their suc-cess was attributed in large part to creatively designed ads.

The pioneers of the new art film movement recognized that the foreign film required a different type of adver-tising than that used for the standard Hollywood production. The primary requirement was an approach which would overcome the stereotype image the public had about foreign films, i.e. they were boring, intellectual or just for dirty old men. The advertising had to legitimize the art film. From the be-ginning the men who dared to import these films knew that they would never have a broad base appeal.

It was understood that these films would attract only a small segment of the movie public—those who considered the film an art form—rather than strictly an entertainment vehicle. The advertising had to reflect this new con-cept. It had to be less flamboyant and more intellectual in its approach. The all-purpose campaign designed to have something for everyone generally used by the industry was definitely un-suitable.

One of the major innovations of the new advertising look was the trend to-ward more white space in the ads. The art film ads lacked the cluttered look usually associated with movie ads. A more classical approach was adopted. The splashy photograph and gobs of copy so prevalent in the ads for Holly-wood productions were dispensed with. The new ads were deceptively simple. The title of the film was prominently displayed on a background of white space and much emphasis was placed on the selection of type face. The art-work was usually a simple pen and ink drawing.

From the beginning, the advertising for foreign films stressed critics' quotes since they were needed to create an aura of respectability. Unlike ads for Hollywood films, the quotes generally remained in context.

Edward Rugoff, his son Donald S. Rugoff, and Walter Reade are credited with being the leaders in instituting some of the sweeping changes which occurred in movie advertising as a result of their efforts in promoting the art film. The idea of the small intimate movie house originated with the elder Rugoff and both Donald Rugoff and Reade developed it. Reade and Don Rugoff had the vision to lease small buildings on the east side of New York before that area had undergone its transformation into a fashionable and desirable location.

Donald Rugoff recognized the importance of advertising and insisted upon the contractual right to approve all advertising artwork used to ballyhoo films at his theatres.

The impact of the new art "movement" on the rest of the industry can be measured by the trend toward cleaner ads for general productions and the decline of the giant movie houses and the subsequent rise of small theatres in shopping centers throughout the country.

Up There—Down There Campaigns

Movie ad lingo includes the phrases *Up There* campaign and *Down There* campaign.

Up There means a campaign appealing to the intellect while Down There means a campaign appealing to the senses. In the jargon of the agencies, Up There appeals to the head—Down There to the groin.

Interestingly, Up There campaigns

are often used for Down There films, such as *I Am Curious, Yellow. Gentlemen's Agreement* was an Up There campaign for an Up There film.

And Down There campaigns are not only used for Down There films (*Gilda, Salome, Miss Sadie Thompson*) but for Up There films, such as Hitchcock's *I Confess.*

Creative Excerpting

For the past fifteen years the film industry has had to contend with the influence of critics.

Before films achieved stature as an art form and were treated strictly as entertainment, reviews lacked real impact. To begin with, the critics were generally confined to only the big city newspapers and the vast majority of the American public was unaware of the critics' reaction, favorable or otherwise. But today, it is not uncommon to have a movie critic on the local weekly and most papers feature movie reviews on a regular basis.

As soon as critics' reviews began to exert an influence on box office receipts, the movie ad industry adopted the practice of prominently quoting the reviewers. Quoting the critics rather than stars and other personalities, such as columnists, grew increasingly common as nationally known critics emerged and people recognized the validity of film criticism.

When a film receives genuinely good reviews there is no problem for the ad department. But for films with mixed or disastrous notices the admen have a practice which is euphemistically known as *creative excerpting*. With this technique the advertising department pores over the dozens of unfavorable reviews and tries to extract one

or two favorable words or phrases.

Many journalists will concede that this is a perfectly valid selling technique—if the comments taken out of context do not distort the critic's intended meaning. But *creative excerpting* refers to those instances where the advertising makes no attempt whatever to preserve the integrity of the original review. With creative or interpretive excerpting there is blatant distortion of the review. The distortion can be accomplished in several ways.

One favorite gambit is to highlight a complimentary adjective used in the review. "Super"—"Fantastic"—"Magnificent"—without telling the reader what the adjective referred to. Was it "a fantastic bore"?

Another common method of distortion is by extracting pieces of sentences from the review and reconstructing them into new thoughts or applying them to other aspects of the picture. *The New York Times* reviews are often victims of this technique. In the reviews for the film *Castle Keep* the critic praised little but the sets. The subsequent ads for the film implied that the *Times* reviewer said the film, not the set, was "extraordinarily beautiful."

When the critic for New York's *CUE* Magazine blasted the film *Song Of Norway*, the ad men were still able to salvage material by using the line "takes up where *Sound Of Music* left off!" The critic seemingly fell right into their attempt to sell the film as a successor to *The Sound Of Music*, but the ads had neglected to carry the complete sentence from the review, which finished with "in the realm of whipped cream entertainment." And the ads carefully avoided mention of the same reviewer's comment that "*Song of Nor-*

way lacked *The Sound of Music's* show business know-how."

There have been some attempts to correct this abuse. At various times prominent critics have publicly attacked the practice and the New York Film Critics Circle investigated the possibility of a legal solution of the problem.

Creative excerpting even attracted the attention of New York City's Commissioner of Consumer Affairs, Bess Myerson Grant. In late 1971, Mrs. Grant announced that her office intended to maintain a close watch on movie ads. She stated that she hoped to use the influence of her office to alleviate the problem of misleading advertising.

Some of the major film distributing companies also feel that they have created a monster with their ads using critics quotes, and in recent years have tried to rectify the situation. Some companies have played down critics' quotes. Other companies have started to use quotes from lesser known reviewers in their ads since they feel too much power often rested with a handful of noted critics like Judith Crist, *The New York Times,* and the star rating system of *The New York Daily News,* along with national magazines like *Time, Newsweek,* and *Life.*

People in the industry note that generally this type of advertising is usually only effective with people who haven't read the reviews. Probably the only hope for reform or outright discontinuation of the practice rests with the ticket buyer. If the industry finds that few people base their decision to see a film on the excerpted testimonials of critics the practice will meet a natural death. This, however, seems unlikely.

Publicity

Publicity is 'free advertising' whereby motion picture companies attempt to garner as much editorial space as possible for their upcoming pictures. Publicity runs the gamut from short news announcements and column blurbs concerning casting, production and release of a film, to interviews with stars, producers, directors, costume designers, screenwriters and anybody else connected with the picture who has the potential of garnering "space."

Publicity departments are responsible for arranging extensive screenings of a film prior to its opening and for starting a word-of-mouth campaign for a picture.

During the good old days when stars were tied to studios by long-term, all-inclusive contracts, publicity was rudimentary. Stars were sent on cross-country tours with intense and detailed publicity schedules. Performers like Judy Garland and Mickey Rooney, under contract to MGM, were even made available to do live stage shows when their pictures opened in major cities like New York.

But today is the day of the free-lance actor, producer, director—each his own boss, and this makes the job of the publicity departments considerably more difficult. It often happens that a film company has no personalities available for publicity in connection with a particular film and must use more obscure members of the cast or behind-the-scenes personalities for publicity purposes.

Publicity has always been considered an important aspect of advertising a film. In many cases editorial space is more valuable and desirable than paid advertising.

Public relations firms have sprung up in the last few years, catering to stars who feel that by using these firms they will get more personal attention. These days a film company's publicity department must often coordinate its activities with public relations agencies when their stars are involved.

Exploitation/Promotion

Of the three types of advertising, exploitation was, in the golden years, Hollywood's forte. In the 1920's, '30's and '40's it offered opportunity for the industry to exhibit its expertise in showmanship, an area in which it has always excelled.

Exploitation, as the very word suggests, is a technique whereby the unique features of a film are "exploited" by the company, for the purpose of garnering additional free publicity and free advertising. Although the ultimate target for exploitation activities is the ticket buyer, the industry utilizes the technique to persuade exhibitors to book their movies. Exhibitors are deluged with suggestions and examples of potential avenues of exploitation designed to create interest in the film.

The importance of exploitation has always been recognized by the industry and all the studios and independent producing companies maintained an exploitation department in conjunction with the advertising department. During the heyday of the big studios, much effort, manpower and expense were allocated for exploitation. For example, MGM, in the late 1930's and '40's, instituted a vast number of programs in this area. A staff of forty highly trained exploitation men or exploiteers (or field men) as they came to be called, covered the entire country and sometimes ventured into other parts of the world. The exploiteers were responsible for contacting the exhibitors in their districts and acted as advisors, helping the theatre owners create advertising campaigns, produce exploitation stunts, and promote civic cooperation. In addition to the services of the exploiteers, MGM published the *Bi-weekly Cooperative Campaign Service* which featured articles and illustrations of exploitation activities utilized by other exhibitors. The service was provided along with the more traditional advance material, like pressbooks.

The exhibitor received recognition through the Honor Roll of Showmen which singled out those theatre owners who had created and produced outstanding campaigns. MGM also ran contests offering big cash prizes to exhibitors who had adapted the studio's suggestions to their own needs and as a result had a successful run.

Exploitation activities may be classified under categories: tie-ins, promotions, civic activities and tours.

A tie-in is merely a technique used by the publicist to tie the movie into a particular product, business or service for the purpose of getting additional free publicity. The tie-in can be a fairly obvious one like arranging with a local furrier to feature the title of the movie *That Touch Of Mink* in all his advertising during the film's run at the local theatre.

At other times, however, the tie-in is a great deal more vague. For example, during a promotional tour for one of his movies, Alfred Hitchcock, a noted wine connoisseur, received free local publicity through a tie-in with a wine company.

Generally, tie-ins have been employed on the road rather than in the big cities. Local merchants have more to

gain by the tie-in than do their big-city counterparts. In addition, this type of advertising is too unsophisticated for national known merchants. On those occasions when tie-ins are used in the metropolitan centers, the film is usually a major production.

Promotion is a general term referring to a wide assortment of activities. Among the more common ones are giveaways of trinkets as mementoes of the film, appearances by the star at supermarket openings and similar occasions and various activities scheduled to coincide with holidays like Mother's Day, Valentine's Day, etc.

Civic activities are usually cooperative ventures undertaken by the exhibitors and the local Chamber of Commerce and similar organizations. Beauty contests, parades, and educational study guides for the films that are distributed free of charge throughout a school system are good examples of this technique.

Another type of exploitation activity is the tour of traveling caravans created by a studio. These tours, if used at all today, are designed for publicizing a specific movie. In former days, big studios would send out tours which emphasized the studio image. The scope of the tours ran the gamut from spectacular extravaganzas like the Trackless Train of MGM that traveled throughout the U.S. and foreign countries, to the more conventional type which might feature a few of the stars who were available for personal appearances at the theatre.

One method of exploitation that has declined in recent years is the use of window cards, handbills and similar visual devices. However, posters are still as effective as ever, but generally their use is prohibited in the very areas ad men would want them displayed.

Consequently, the practice of wildcat posting has sprung up in most major cities. Naturally, since the practice is illegal, the agencies and movie companies cannot do the posting themselves. However, there are people who are hired to put up the posters.

Exploitation is not as popular today as it used to be. No longer do the studios employ separate staffs responsible for its execution. If there are exploitation activities they are handled by the regular advertising and publicity department.

Several factors contributed to the decline of exploitation. The studios could no longer justify the expense after the number of annual productions had decreased. The trend toward fewer stars under contract prevented the studios from being able to guarantee their appearance at the various activities. The whole connotation of the word exploitation was distasteful and as greater segments of the population have become more affluent, more urbanized and more sophisticated, the practice has now lost most of its appeal.

In-House Vs. Agency

When the studios were flourishing, most if not all advertising efforts were produced by an in-house staff. Complete campaigns were devised by the studio departments. The companies produced their own trailers, created their own art work for the ads, placed the ads, and handled all publicity and exploitation activities. Movie moguls like Harry Cohn and David O. Selznick were active participants in this phase of the industry, and the campaigns for their films implemented many of their ideas.

Many of the studios developed a

unique advertising image which was repeated in all their ads. Although the ads were geared to individual pictures, care was taken to enhance the studio image. The stars were used as selling points and it was not unusual to have the ad subtly remind the moviegoer that it was Warner Brothers who had Jimmy Cagney under contract.

Today, outside advertising agencies are responsible for creating the bulk of the campaigns used in paid advertising. Several factors are responsible for the curtailment of in-house departments. When the eight major studios accounted for the great majority of the total number of productions released annually, these companies could well afford the cost of an extensive in-house staff. However, as the era of the studios faded, and small independent producers and distributors came to the fore, the need and the expense of internal departments was no longer justified.

The complexities involved in placing the ads—or media-buying, as it is called within the industry—also hastened the trend toward the use of outside agencies. These big agencies which service many clients are able to perform this aspect of the job far more efficiently. This part of the business grew in significance as the use of radio and TV spots increased and the studios discontinued the practice of having numerous offices (exchanges) located throughout the country.

Although the agencies are capable of developing the entire ad campaign, some moviemakers create their own original artwork which they submit to the agency for execution and placing. Ad agencies seldom earn a profit on the creative part of the business. Their money is made in the execution, media-buying and placement areas.

As the number of productions re-leased on an annual basis declined, as the contract system for stars became a relic of the past, and as the financial risks inherent in the industry escalated, it became far more important to develop campaigns which emphasized an individual film. No longer, except in the case of Disney, were the campaigns designed to reinforce the studio image. The ads had to reflect the changes in the industry as well as the changes in the public's attitudes toward films. An outside agency was more apt to approach the task with objectivity than an in-house staff bred on old practices. However, the producers and other persons high in the corporate structure still reserved the right to veto or approve the ad campaigns. That part of the business had not changed.

The boutique idea used for the independent production of trailers carries over into the creation of entire advertising campaigns—one shop may create the artwork for print media, another for radio and tv, and still another may do all the media buying and placement.

Although moviemakers often use regular consumer advertising agencies, there are several firms specializing in the movie field. The man credited with establishing the first separate advertising agency geared specifically to servicing the film industry is Monroe Greenthal, who was a noted film buff. He recognized that the industry had its own unique needs and that the more traditional types of advertising agencies were incapable of providing the services which it required. Today, the company he founded, now Diener/Hauser/Greenthal, is considered one of the leaders in the field. Among other leading agencies are the Charles Schlaifer Agency and W. H. Schneider, Inc.

Coming Attractions

Trailers is the trade name for the *coming attraction* film clips. They have always been widely used by the industry for they offer several advantages unavailable with more traditional modes of advertising.

Undoubtedly, their single greatest advantage is the assurance they provide the movie maker that he is reaching his intended target—the potential moviegoer. It is estimated that between forty and fifty percent of the audience for a particular movie has seen the trailer. Another beneficial characteristic of the trailer is that unlike a newspaper ad or billboard it does not have to compete for the audience's attention. The captive audience is an ad man's utopia. In addition to these advantages, the cost of this method of advertising is relatively low, since the most sizable expenditure is the initial charge of production. If calculated on a per showing basis and measured against the more standard forms of reaching the ticketbuyer, a trailer represents a good value.

One of the ironies of the movie business is that often in the past, as a result of creative editing, the trailers were far more exciting than the actual film. When the studios had tight release schedules the trailers generally had to be produced before the completed version of the film survived ordeal of the cutting room—hence the trailer sometimes carried scenes not in the final cut.

For many years the studios produced their own trailers. Some unsophisticated moviegoers used to believe that the theatre owner himself cut scenes from the film to produce the short. National Screen Service Corporation, the major factor in the trailer business now, is the only company that distributes its product on a national basis. In addition to the trailers, National Screen Service co-produces various other promotional aids. Each theatre owner is offered a package of over ten items for marquee and theatre display.

The concept of the trailer has undergone many changes through the years. During the silent era, the trailer often consisted of a slide or a series of slides flashed on the screen. As the medium grew more sophisticated and the benefits to such direct advertising became more readily apparent, more care was lavished on the production of the coming attraction shorts. As the importance of the trailer became more widely recognized, the use of outside sources became more prevalent. Today the production of trailers and their offshoot, the super-trailers or the so-called featurettes, has become a separate industry.

The featurette, or one or two-reel short, produced to sell a particular movie is considered the fastest growing segment of the film advertising business. It differs from the more conventional trailer since it consists of more than excerpts from the movie. The featurette resembles a documentary in tone though its primary purpose is to sell the specific film. Often the featurette depicts behind-the-scenes activities, as well as capturing the complexities involved in producing a film. The director and the co-stars are often the subjects of lengthy interviews probing the meaning of the film and the underlying concepts governing decisions regarding interpretation, acting, photography, etc.

One of the unique aspects of the featurette is that unlike trailers which are produced solely to be shown in theatres

the new super-trailers are shown on television. They sometimes appear after the numerous Movie Of The Week programs on network television. The producers of the movie provide the featurette to television stations throughout the country *gratis* and it is considered a major coup if one is accepted for showing during prime time on network T.V.

Another characteristic of the featurette is that it is designed to provide a soft-sell approach, unlike its prototype, the theatre trailer, which makes no pretensions concerning its ultimate purpose.

As in other areas of advertising, the trend toward small creative shops (boutiques) has extended to the making of trailers. And the advent of featurettes has provided further impetus for these boutiques. There are numerous little companies which produce only trailers and featurettes. And many people in the industry feel that some of the most creative filmmaking is in this area.

Teaser Ads

Teaser ads are one of the more provocative selling tools used by the industry. They are usually run immediately prior to a film's opening and are created to arouse the reader or listener's curiosity. Unlike standard ads, they reveal a minimum amount of information. Very often they will appear in non-entertainment sections of the paper.

Two of the most effective teaser ads of all are: "The Birds Is Coming," used for Hitchcock's 1966 thriller *The Birds,* and "Remember The Day The 7th Of May," for *Duel In The Sun* in 1947.

Awards

The uniqueness of movie advertising, as distinguished from consumer advertising was recognized in 1969 with the establishment of the Annual Motion Picture Advertising Awards, sponsored by the B'nai B'rith Cinema Lodge. All aspects of the business of selling a movie are covered and over twelve separate categories represent the different areas.

The categories include: Best campaign, ad, copy-line, theatrical trailer, logo, trade ad, radio spot, poster, review ad, teaser ads, tv spot, painting, photo.

The panel of over twenty distinguished advertising executives and craftsmen, some of whom are members of the industry, select five finalists for each category. Awards are given to each finalist with the top entry receiving a Grand Award. According to the rules of the Awards, judges are to base their decisions on the following criteria: Attention getting, distinctive, creative, believable, compelling, provocative and likely to motivate those people seeing or hearing them to see the motion picture they advertise.

The Director As Star

Just as stars were key selling factors for films, so, in certain cases, were directors and producers.

In the early 1900's, D. W. Griffith was the first director to explore the film medium as an art form, and his name became a boxoffice magnet. Although he followed *Birth of a Nation* (1915) with another spectacle, *Intolerance,* Griffith, unlike other directors, resisted being typed. He continued his career by making dramas, comedies, mysteries. His forte was quality films and in ads emphasis was placed on the fact that it was A Griffith Production. Stars were never highlighted. Advertising for Griffith films was classically simple, merely an announcement that the new Griffith movie was being released.

As the slide for *The Squaw Man* (1919) illustrates, even then Cecil B. DeMille's name was used as the drawing card in advertising his films. His silent version of *The Ten Commandments* was a huge success and by the time his production of *The Sign of the Cross* was released in 1932, DeMille's name had become synonymous with the "epic." As a result, advertising for one of his films simply had to inform the audience that the movie was a DeMille production.

In the early '30's, the name of director Frank Capra became trademark. He received top billing over the title and over the stars. He had become so associated with a certain type of movie (comedies with a "message") that the phrase "The Capra Touch" was coined. (Some people derisively referred to it as Capra-corn.)

For many years, Capra's movies were the only "A" films produced by Columbia Pictures. Consequently, in ads, his name was spotlighted in order to differentiate his films from other Columbia productions. And to exploit his long string of successes, the advertising frequently mentioned his past hits.

Unlike Griffith, DeMille and Capra, who combined producing and directing, but were noted for their directorial expertise, some men achieved fame for being solely producers, albeit creative in all phases of film's production. In such a context, David O. Selznick became famous. His career spanned three decades and included stints as head of production at RKO Pictures and head of his own unit at MGM. Through the late '30's and '40's, he turned to independent production and became his own distributor.

Selznick, like Griffith, did not confine himself to any specific type of film but won acclaim for the high calibre of his movies. After *Gone with the Wind*, his name became as important in selling his movies as the names of the stars in the films. Seldom did ads for Selznick movies fail to mention the fact that he was the producer of *Gone with the Wind*.

Unlike Griffith, Selznick was star-conscious, as evidenced by the ad for *Since You Went Away*, which lists seven stars but of course has Selznick's name above them all!

Through the years there have been other producer-director boxoffice draws—William Wyler, Otto Preminger, John Ford, Elia Kazan, to mention a few. In recent years David Lean (*Lawrence of Arabia, Dr. Zhivago, Bridge on the River Kwai, Ryan's Daughter*) has established himself as a director whose name is known to the public and draws an audience. Director Billy Wilder, on the heels of his successes *Some Like It Hot* and *The Apartment*, was the focal point of the ad campaign for *One, Two, Three*, although the film starred James Cagney.

GREAT MOMENT from a Great Love Story!

The Story of a Great Detective Who Didn't Know He Was Trailing His Own Heartbreak!

Brought to the screen by William Wyler, Academy Award Winner who gave you "The Best Years of Our Lives"... and Pulitzer Prize Winner Sidney Kingsley, author of "Dead End"... and featuring members of the cast that made the Broadway play so sensational!

"I'm sorry, Jim...
I never said
I was a saint!"

KIRK
DOUGLAS
ELEANOR
PARKER
WILLIAM
BENDIX

in WILLIAM WYLER'S
PRODUCTION OF SIDNEY KINGSLEY'S
Detective Story
FROM THE SMASH STAGE SUCCESS!

Also starring
CATHY
O'DONNELL · Produced and Directed by WILLIAM WYLER · Screenplay by PHILIP YORDAN and
ROBERT WYLER · Based on the play by SIDNEY KINGSLEY · A Paramount Picture

In The John Ford Tradition of Greatness

John Ford and Merian C. Cooper
present

JOHN WAYNE
JOANNE DRU
JOHN AGAR
BEN JOHNSON
HARRY CAREY, Jr.

in

JOHN WAYNE
in his most heroic role as
Captain Brittles of the
U.S. Cavalry.

She Wore a Yellow Ribbon

with VICTOR McLAGLEN
MILDRED NATWICK · GEORGE O'BRIEN
ARTHUR SHIELDS

Directed by JOHN FORD

Story by JAMES WARNER BELLAH
Screen Play by FRANK NUGENT and LAURENCE STALLINGS

COLOR BY TECHNICOLOR

Produced by ARGOSY PICTURES CORPORATION   Distributed by RKO RADIO PICTURES

| JOANNE DRU as Olivia | JOHN AGAR as Lt. Cohill | BEN JOHNSON as Tyree | HARRY CAREY, Jr. as Lt. Pennell | VICTOR McLAGLEN as Sgt. Quincannon | GEORGE O'BRIEN as Maj. Allshard |

The Director As Star

By the 1960's, foreign as well as American directors had accumulated auteur followings. Cults sprung up in key cities for various directors and film revivals became a way of life for some. The boxoffice draw of certain directors was tremendous (Fellini, Antonioni, etc.). Others had a small and steady following (Godard, Bunuel, Truffaut).

Alfred Hitchcock, from his earliest films imported from Britain to his first films made in America *(Rebecca, Suspicion, Shadow of a Doubt)*, has been associated with suspense movies. By the middle of the 1950's, his immense popularity and years of being billed as the "Master Of Suspense" had made him as big a boxoffice draw as any star. He gained additional popularity with his successful TV series and reached the peak of his movie fame in 1960 with the release of *Psycho*. By that time Hitchock had become so noted for suspense that Paramount was able to sell the film virtually on the basis of the Hitchcock name alone.

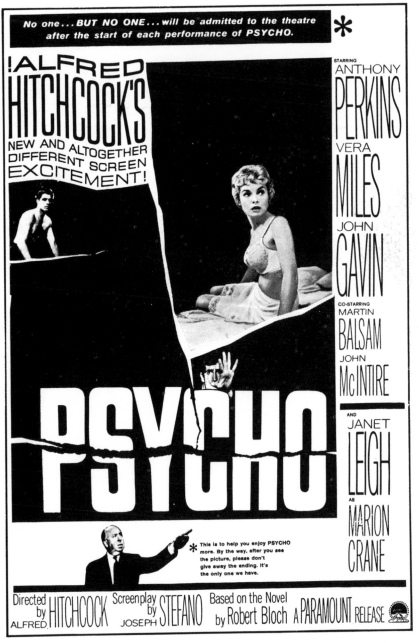

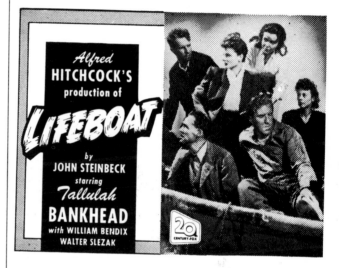

Alfred
HITCHCOCK'S
production of
LIFEBOAT
by
JOHN STEINBECK
starring
Tallulah
BANKHEAD
with WILLIAM BENDIX
WALTER SLEZAK
20 CENTURY-FOX

THIS IS BILLY WILDER. HE MADE 'THE
APARTMENT' & 'SOME LIKE IT HOT.'
NOW—HIS EXPLOSIVE NEW COMEDY,

ONE, TWO, THREE

IT STARS: JAMES CAGNEY, HORST BUCHHOLZ,
PAMELA TIFFIN, ARLENE FRANCIS

CO-STARRING:
HOWARD ST. JOHN HANNS LOTHAR & LILO PULVER

FILMED IN PANAVISION® SCREEN PLAY BY BILLY WILDER AND I.A.L. DIAMOND · PRODUCED AND DIRECTED
BY BILLY WILDER · MUSIC ADAPTED AND CONDUCTED BY ANDRÉ PREVIN · PRESENTED BY THE MIRISCH
COMPANY INC. IN ASSOCIATION WITH PYRAMID PRODUCTIONS, A.G. · RELEASED THROUGH UNITED ARTISTS

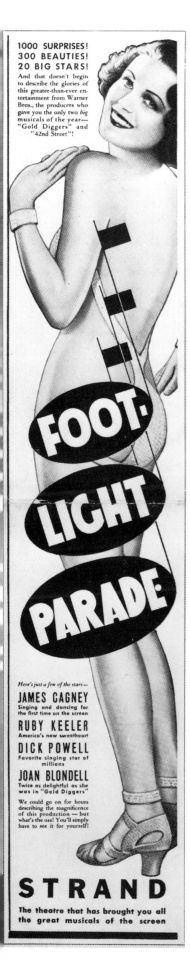

Do You Remember?

132

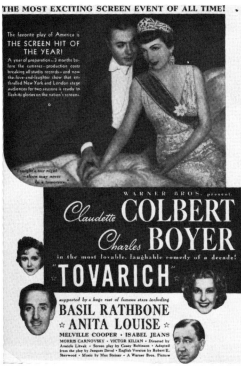

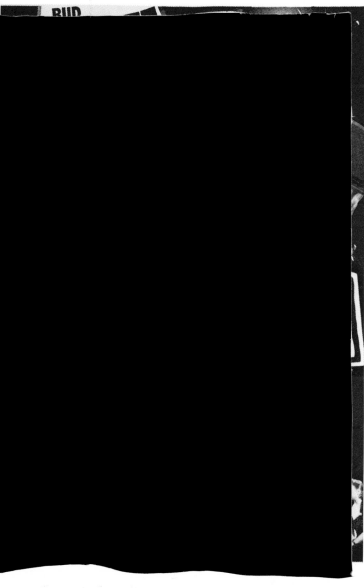

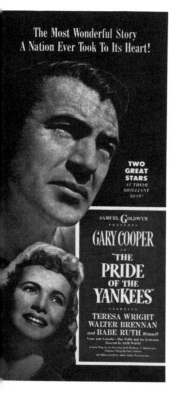

The Most Wonderful Story
A Nation Ever Took To Its Heart!

TWO GREAT STARS AT THEIR BRILLIANT BEST!

SAMUEL GOLDWYN PRESENTS

GARY COOPER
IN
"THE PRIDE OF THE YANKEES"

STARRING
TERESA WRIGHT
WALTER BRENNAN
and BABE RUTH Himself

UNIVERSAL'S
SUPREME CHAPTER-PLAY

IN THE DAYS of
DANIEL BOONE

featuring
JACK MOWER
AND
EILEEN SEDGWICK
WITH A BIG SUPPORTING CAST

BY JEFFERSON MOFFIT

DIRECTED BY
FRANK MESSINGER AND JAY MARCHANT

Big, Bouncy and Beautiful On the Big Screen!

Smoo-oo-th as silk—joy-o-o-ous is the word for it! Everything that made the two-year Broadway hit a smash attraction sparkles with ten-fold brilliance in M-G-M's high, wide and Cole Porter entertainment!

with wonderful Cole Porter songs!

"THE RITZ ROLL AND ROCK"
"PARIS LOVES LOVERS"
"SATIN AND SILK"
"HAIL BIBINSKI"
"STEREOPHONIC SOUND"
"ALL OF YOU"
and others!

M-G-M presents AN ARTHUR FREED PRODUCTION starring

FRED ASTAIRE · CYD CHARISSE
IN
Silk Stockings

also co-starring
JANIS PAIGE · PETER LORRE
with JULES MUNSHIN · GEORGE TOBIAS · JOSEPH BULOFF
Screen Play by LEONARD GERSHE and LEONARD SPIGELGASS
Suggested by "Ninotchka" by Melchior Lengyel · Music and Lyrics by COLE PORTER
Book of Original Musical Play by GEORGE S. KAUFMAN,
LEUEEN McGRATH and ABE BURROWS
Produced on the stage by Cy Feuer and Ernest H. Martin
in CinemaScope and Metrocolor · Directed by ROUBEN MAMOULIAN

Treat Yourself to a Double Exposure of Fun and Foolishness!

DOUBLE DYNAMITE!
starring
JANE RUSSELL · GROUCHO MARX
FRANK SINATRA

TNT TUNES!
"IT'S ONLY MONEY"
"KISSES AND TEARS"

RKO RADIO

Directed by IRVING CUMMINGS · Produced by IRVING CUMMINGS, JR.
Screenplay by MELVILLE SHAVELSON · Story by LEO ROSTEN

Sequels and Series

When a film is successful, its producers often decide, if circumstances permit, to make a sequel—or at least a successor—to capitalize on the popularity of the first film. Briefly, there are four kinds of sequels.

The first type of sequel—same characters, same setting, and continuing the story where the last film ended—was often very successful. For example, *Father's Little Dividend*, which followed *Father of the Bride*.

Some sequels will use the same character but in new situations—Mr. Belvedere, Clifton Webb's famous character, was introduced in a film called *Sitting Pretty*. In ensuing films, titles were along the lines: *Mr. Belvedere Goes to College*, etc.

Metro-Goldwyn-Mayer Presents

JUDGE HARDY & SON
with
LEWIS STONE · MICKEY ROONEY
CECILIA PARKER · FAY HOLDEN
Original Story and Screen Play by Carey Wilson
Directed by George B. Seitz

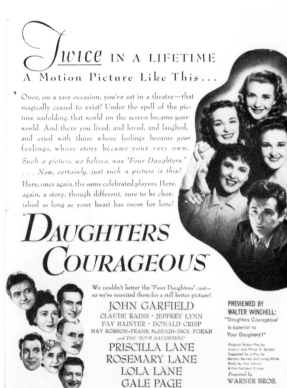

Another type of sequel takes the same actors—who clicked in a particular film—and puts them in another similarly plotted film. Bing Crosby and Barry Fitzgerald were heartwarming priests in the successful *Going My Way*. So Paramount made them heartwarming doctors in *Welcome Stranger*.

Finally there is the successor—not exactly a sequel. In this case the same actors are used, but the plot is not continued on from the original, it is changed slightly. For example, Warner Brothers decided to capitalize on the popularity of stars and story in *Four Daughters* and soon after produced *Daughters Courageous*. *Daughters Courageous* in turn had a more direct sequel (fewer change and the characters remained the same), *Four Wives*.

Series are of two types: When the characters originate from another medium (such as the detective or spy series' James Bond, The Saint, Sherlock Holmes, Boston Blackie, Charlie Chan, etc.); and when the popularity of certain films warrant continued sequels— Andy Hardy, Ma and Pa Kettle, Francis The Talking Mule, and the ape characters introduced in *Planet of the Apes*.

Paramount's *Road* pictures are interesting because the three stars Bing Crosby, Bob Hope and Dorothy Lamour, always played essentially the same characters, though their names changed and naturally locales were different from film to film.

In almost all advertising for sequels and series the film companies stress the popularity and success of the previous film: "See Them Together Again..."; "Picks Up Where——Left Off..."; "Funnier Than——..." and similar tag lines. As in remakes and reissues, when films in a series click, they are often remarketed in tandem.

In addition, sequels are often titled *Son of...* or *Return to...* or *Return of*. When Errol Flynn's son Sean portrayed

The Son of Captain Blood—the original *Captain Blood* had starred Errol—Sean was billed as "The Son of Errol Flynn."

It's also interesting to note that as series continued, the billing of certain actors often changed. Lewis Stone got top billing over Mickey Rooney for many years in the Andy Hardy series. Dorothy Lamour got second billing in her first *Road* movie with Bing and Bob, but she was billed third in ensuing *Road* films. John Garfield, way down in billing in *Four Daughters*, was top-billed thereafter.

It is generally assumed by the industry that sequels will not be as successful as the original, but a second film, if produced inexpensively, will reap a decent profit. *Valley of the Dolls* was such a financially successful book and film that 20th Century-Fox decided on a sequel. But the second film, *Beyond the Valley of the Dolls*, fell far short of expectations. However, 20th had an extraordinary experience with its film *Planet of the Apes* and its two sequels, *Beneath the Planet of the Apes* and *Return to Planet of the Apes*. Each film in the series was more successful than its predecessor.

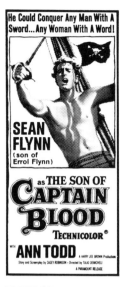

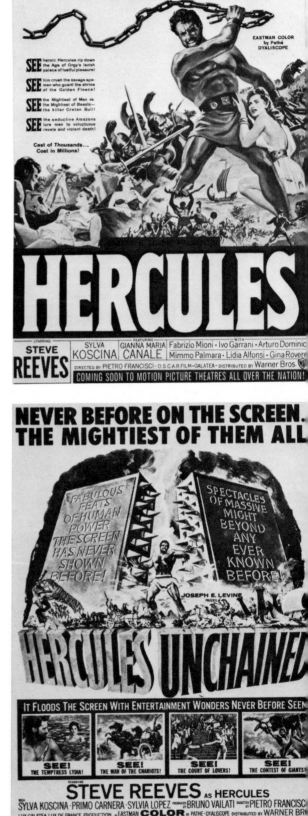

THE NATIONS MOST STARTLING AND
HOTLY DISCUSSED BEST-SELLER NOW
ON THE SCREEN WITH EVERY SHOCK
AND SENSATION INTACT!

Valley of the Dolls

Any similarity
between
any person,
living or dead,
and the
characters
portrayed
in this film
is purely
coincidental
and not
intended.

20th CENTURY-FOX Presents A MARK ROBSON·DAVID WEISBART PRODUCTION
STARRING
BARBARA PARKINS·PATTY DUKE·PAUL BURKE·SHARON TATE·
GUEST STARS
TONY SCOTTI·LEE GRANT |JOEY BISHOP·GEORGE JESSEL|
SUSAN HAYWARD as Helen Lawson
Produced by DAVID WEISBART · Directed by MARK ROBSON · Screenplay by HELEN DEUTSCH and DOROTHY KINGSLEY
Songs by DORY and ANDRE PREVIN·Based on a Book by JACQUELINE SUSANN · DIONNE WARWICK sings the theme from "Valley of the Dolls"
PANAVISION· COLOR by DeLUXE · ORIGINAL SOUND TRACK ALBUM ON 20th CENTURY-FOX RECORDS

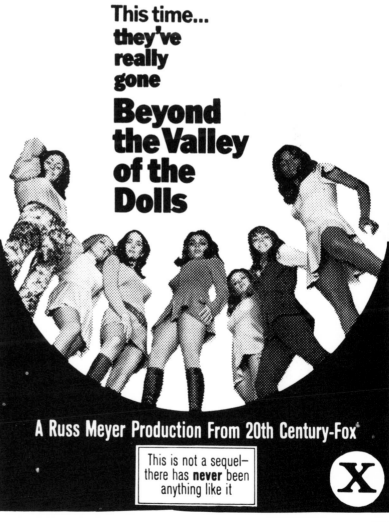

This time...
they've
really
gone
**Beyond
the Valley
of the
Dolls**

A Russ Meyer Production From 20th Century-Fox

This is not a sequel—
there has **never** been
anything like it

X

Music and the Movies

From the earliest days, film companies have made promotional tie-ins with the music industry. Often film companies owned and published their own music. They reaped additional advertising for their films via sheet music and, later on, record labels and album covers.

Sheet music, which was popular throughout the 1940's, was often used for display because scenes from the film, or photos of the stars, could be used to illustrate the song from the particular film. Often, a star was highlighted, although no particular film was plugged *(Sippin' Cider Through a Straw)*.

In the 1930's and '40's, long before LP albums became a staple, film companies had to settle for plugging their films with simple credit lines on the labels of records—"as sung by Judy Garland in MGM's *Broadway Melody of 1938*"—"as featured in 20th Century-Fox's *Pigskin Parade*."

The popularity of LP albums and the establishment of record company subsidiaries allowed the movie companies to capitalize on the lucrative market for movie soundtracks.

The profits made on the music from films have been enormous and from an advertising and promotion point of view, album jackets, ads for the albums and the success of the music (air play and reference to the film) have provided millions of dollars in free advertising.

Misleading Ad Lines

Although the industry today is pretty much true to the concept that the most important task of the ad man is to honestly portray the essence of a film for the audience, it was not too unusual during the 1930's and '40's, and even the '50's, to find ads that were misleading. The ads were misleading in various ways, and, in retrospect, are often amusing.

Probably the most common offense was the subtle manner in which the subject matter of certain films was either never referred to or described in terms which were at best ambiguous. The photograph which accompanied the ad for the 1945 John Garfield starrer, *Pride of the Marines*, represents a good example of Hollywood's fear that certain subjects had to be played down out of consideration for the audience's sensibilities. Despite the fact that

John GARFIELD
Eleanor PARKER
Dane CLARK
PRIDE OF THE MARINES
Warner Bros.

Directed by DELMER DAVES • Screen Play by ALBERT MALTZ • Adaptation by Marvin Borowsky • From a Book by Roger Butterfield • Music by FRANZ WAXMAN
Produced by JERRY WALD

ride of the Marines concerned the plight of a man blinded in
World War II and his subsequent adjustment to his blindness, some
ds for the film resembled those for a bright, breezy musical. They were
esigned to convey a mood of gaiety and happiness, and there was
bsolutely no reference to the tragedy in the story, either implicit
explicit.

The advertising for Stanley Kramer's 1950 film, *The Men*,
as an example of another instance when the producers shied away
rom mentioning the subject matter of the movie. In this story
arlon Brando was a paraplegic confined to a wheelchair. Not only
d the key ad art and the ad line—"A Completely New Experience
etween Men and Women"—fail to allude to the chief character's
lemma, but it created an entirely false impression of sensationalism.

Note the ad for the 1945 blockbuster, *The Bells of St. Mary's*. It leads the reader to believe that the movie is a love story rather than about a heartwarming relationship between a priest and a nun.

The entire tone of the ad for the 1956 drama, *Storm Center*, is ambiguous, starting with the line, "Who *Really* Set the Town Aflame?" The implication that Bette Davis is the center of a controversy involving something of a sexual nature could not be more misleading. The film is really about a middle-aged small-town librarian, portrayed by Bette, who refuses to bow to political pressure and book burning.

Such blatant attempts to mislead were more infrequent than ads which emphasized the less significant aspects of a movie. The ads for *The Best Years of Our Lives* and *Our Town* fall into this category. Although the themes were serious, the ad men chose to exploit the love story angle.

The ads for the 1954 John Huston film, *Beat the Devil* are interesting because, on completion of the movie, the producers, who had expected an adventure film, were somewhat flabbergasted to find instead an off-beat satiric comedy. They assumed the public wasn't expecting Humphrey Bogart, Jennifer Jones and Gina Lollobrigida to be in an off-beat comedy. So the film was given an "adventure" advertising campaign, standard for a Bogart action movie. But the public was wising up. The film flopped.

Selling the Trade

To impress exhibitors, the big studios published
extensive campaign books of high quality. In 1925, the major
studios were emerging and Paramount was one of the top
in the industry. Paramount wanted the exhibitors to know
that it had lined up an array of stars and product which
was going to be difficult to match. Books such as this have
become highly sought collector's items.

BOX OFFICE NAMES in *Paramount's* SHOWMAN'S PICTURES

Where but in Paramount can you match a list like this?

PARAMOUNT STOCK COMPANY

STARS AND ARTISTS

GLORIA SWANSON	THOMAS MEIGHAN	POLA NEGRI
RICHARD DIX	BEBE DANIELS	RAYMOND GRIFFITH
ADOLPHE MENJOU	BETTY BRONSON	DOUGLAS MAC LEAN
JACK HOLT	LOIS WILSON	RICARDO CORTEZ
FLORENCE VIDOR	PERCY MARMONT	ALICE JOYCE
BILLIE DOVE	CAROL DEMPSTER	GRETA NISSEN
MARY BRIAN	ERNEST TORRENCE	WILLIAM COLLIER, Jr.
WALLACE BEERY	W. C. FIELDS	ESTHER RALSTON
WARNER BAXTER	NEIL HAMILTON	NOAH BEERY
RAYMOND HATTON	LAWRENCE GRAY	FORD STERLING
BESSIE LOVE	HARRISON FORD	TOM MOORE
LIONEL BARRYMORE	GEORGE BANCROFT	GERTRUDE ASTOR
NORMAN TREVOR	ARTHUR EDMUND CAREWE	MARC McDERMOTT
CONWAY TEARLE	WILLIAM POWELL	CLARA BOW
GEORGE RIGAS	RICHARD ARLEN	LILA LEE
ALYCE MILLS	DONALD KEITH	GILBERT ROWLAND

DIRECTORS

JAMES CRUZE	HERBERT BRENON	ALLAN DWAN
RAOUL WALSH	MALCOLM ST. CLAIR	FRANK TUTTLE
IRVIN WILLAT	VICTOR FLEMING	CLARENCE BADGER
WILLIAM HOWARD	GEORGE SEITZ	VICTOR HEERMAN
EDWARD SUTHERLAND	GREGORY LA CAVA	LEONCE PERRET
WILLIAM DE MILLE	ROBERT FLAHERTY	MERIAN COOPER

SUPERVISORS

HECTOR TURNBULL	BEN SCHULBERG	WILLIAM LE BARON
LUCIEN HUBBARD	LLOYD SHELDON	TOWNSEND MARTIN
LUTHER REED	TOM GERAGHTY	JULIAN JOHNSON
WALTER WOODS	ROY POMEROY	JOHN LYNCH
WILLIS GOLDBECK	GARRET WESTEN	KENNETH HAWKS

AUTHORS IN THIS GROUP OF PICTURES

ZANE GREY	GEORGE M. COHAN	FANNIE HURST
GEO. BARR McCUTCHEON	BYRON MORGAN	MICHAEL ARLEN
RING LARDNER	ROBERT SHERWOOD	ALFRED SAVOIR
HUGH WILEY	FRANCIS YOUNG	H. A. DU SOUCHET
GERALD BEAUMONT	LAWRENCE EYRE	EDGAR SELWYN
LEO DITRICHSTEIN	MAURICE SAMUELS	MONTE KATTERJOHN

And They're All Paramount!

Exclusive of Stars (*The Greatest Stars in Motion Pictures*) *Three Box Office Names will be in each* Paramount's SHOWMAN'S PICTURE *to be cast from this list of* DISTINGUISHED ARTISTS *in* Paramount's STOCK COMPANY

EXCLUSIVE OF STARS

WHAT a tremendous treasure-trove of names is contained in that list of the Paramount Stock Company.
From that Golconda will be mined the names that go
into the rich structure of each of the pictures listed in
this book. The value of box-office names in big pictures
was never more evident than today.

Paramount is in a better position than ever in the history of the screen, to capitalize on the need for public-pulling names that draw the crowds to the ticket window.

Paramount advertising, Paramount publicity, the
true genius of the artists themselves have combined to
make those names stand for the most popular men and
women in all the world. They are the great personalities who will be called on to enrich the tremendous
stories provided in the pictures listed in this group.

Exhibitors may rest assured that each and every one
of these pictures will be recruited with names that
really mean something to the public today.

Look them over, compare them with all the available
talent and genius in pictures today.

Where, but in Paramount, can you match a list like this?

The swiftest, most exciting race story ever written by the speed-story writer, Byron Morgan...

For thrills it has

A SENSATIONAL smash of a giant sea-plane! An amazing race between a speed boat and the Havana Express across the Florida Keys! A breath-taking race in fashionable Miami between the fastest speed boats in the world—a race in which Bebe herself takes part, having risked fortune and happiness for the sake of winning!

'THE PALM BEACH GIRL'

ON the front pages of every newspaper you see Florida, Palm Beach, society girls on the sand, bathing beauties, wealth, spice, gaiety, speed. This is the atmosphere of the fastest of all Bebe Daniels comedies, "The Palm Beach Girl." Bebe plays the girl, rich, beautiful, wooed by many men. Apparently bored and blasé, but actually daring and eager for thrills. Pell-mell into the funniest and wildest turmoil of adventures possible she falls, and before she's through she's got the audience breathless from laughter and excitement.

The top notch double barreled AA No. 1 of long-run specials!

This, LADIES AND GENTLEMEN - is

HAROLD LLOYD

THE most remarkable figure in the history of motion pictures. In his name alone, without a doubt, the most stupendous box-office draw in the world today. To analyze the reasons for that fact would be to recount the whole history of all the painstaking efforts his corporation makes to produce for the American public the exact thing that the public wants.

And that is what he (and they) have done in Harold Lloyd's first release under the Paramount banner.

It's difficult to improve past performances that seem perfect

But the actual truth is "For Heaven's Sake" is Harold Lloyd's best picture

a Paramount Picture

in "FOR HEAVEN'S SAKE!"

TWO OF THE SEASON'S GREATEST COMEDY LONG-RUN SPECIALS..

"IT'S THE OLD ARMY GAME!"

Starring

W. C. FIELDS

FOR years W. C. Fields had a de luxe comedy juggling act in the Follies in which he was amazingly funny without uttering a word. Given his first speaking part, in the musical comedy "Poppy," he was the over-night sensation of Broadway! Night after night, for over a year, he stopped the show. His tag-line, "It's the Old Army Game!" became a part of the language.

When D. W. Griffith filmed "Sally of the Sawdust," he introduced the marvellous pantomimic gifts of Fields to the motion picture world. Paramount thus is able to offer you the first Fields starring special, "It's the Old Army Game!", built around the great comedy character created by Fields—that of the lovable flim-flammer who "never gives a sucker an even break."

A Paramount Picture

"FRESH PAINT"

Starring

RAYMOND GRIFFITH

TO EXHIBITORS: Raymond Griffith is your star. You discovered him. You urged us to star him. Long before we actually did star him, you were playing him up as a star in your advertising and publicity. We promised to help you by starring him in big comedy specials made by as an elaborate and as fine a comedy organization as could be gotten together. We kept our promise, as you know, in "A Regular Fellow." We are keeping it again in the new Griffith comedy "Hands Up!" We are going to do more than keep our promise in "Fresh Paint."

We are planning to shoot the whole works on Griffith in "Fresh Paint!" We are going to give you the greatest laughter-entertainment that will put Raymond Griffith where he doesn't have to take off his famous high hat to any other comedian on the screen, bar none!

A Paramount Picture

THREE MORE OF PARAMOUNT'S LONG-RUN SPECIALS

'VOLCANO!'

℞ *for the box-office*

BEBE Daniels, as Zabette
RICARDO Cortez, of "Pony Express" fame
WALLACE Beery, a real box-office draw
WILLIAM Howard, who made "The Thundering Herd"
LOVE, thrills, action, spectacle, volcano

'THE GRAND DUCHESS AND THE WAITER'

℞ *for the box-office*

ADOLPHE Menjou's greatest role
FLORENCE Vidor and Parisian clothes.
MALCOLM St. Clair, the new "genius" director
ANDRE de Beranger, of "Are Parents People?"
LAUGHS, romance, excitement, consummate acting

"DANCING MOTHERS"

℞ *for the box-office*

CONWAY Tearle as the father
ALICE Joyce as the mother
BETTY Bronson as the daughter
HERBERT Brenon as the director
WILLIAM Collier, Jr., of "Wanderer" fame
TEARS and heart-tugs, laughs and thrills

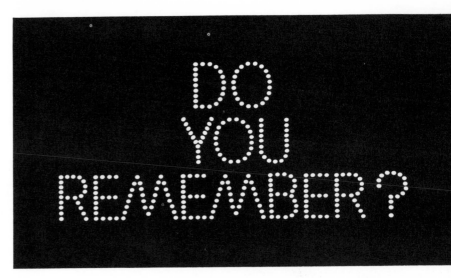

168

woodstock the movie
(with a little help from our friends.)

starring joan baez · joe cocker · country joe & the fish · crosby, stills, nash & young · arlo guthrie · richie havens · jimi hendrix
santana · john sebastian · sha-na-na · sly & the family stone · ten years after · the who · and 400,000 other beautiful people.

a film by michael wadleigh · produced by bob maurice
a wadleigh-maurice, ltd. production · technicolor® from warner bros.

NO PICTURE HAS EVER EQUALLED "CONQUEST"!

GRETA GARBO
CHARLES BOYER

IN CLARENCE BROWN'S PRODUCTION

Conquest

THE LOVE STORY OF MARIE WALEWSKA

Even Metro-Goldwyn-Mayer—with the greatest productions in motion picture history to its credit—has never before made a picture on so lavish a scale as this. Its grandeur will dazzle your eyes...as its romance fills your heart. Garbo, as the temptress who is used to ensnare Charles Boyer as Napoleon; a glorious seductive pawn in an amazing international intrigue. A cast of thousands including Reginald Owen, Alan Marshall, Henry Stephenson, Leif Erickson, Dame May Whitty, C. Henry Gordon. Directed by Clarence Brown. Produced by Bernard H. Hyman...Screen Play by Samuel Hoffenstein, Salka Viertel and S. N. Behrman.

A GIANT PRODUCTION IN THE BRILLIANT M·G·M MANNER

Kipling's heroic lines inspire Hollywood's biggest movie!

Out of the drumbeat rhythm of Kipling's most famous 85 lines rises a picture that may well become known as the one great MOVIE of the year!...Big on the score of its armies in battle, its war elephants, its bandit hordes, its terror Temples and mystic mountains of India...Bigger still in its scope and sweep, its thrill and action...But biggest of all in the life it breathes through three roaring, reckless, swaggering sons of the thundering guns...fightin' men who stride its mighty scenes in the flesh and blood of high adventure—it is the honest movie of it all that makes Gunga Din a new experience in entertainment.

GUNGA DIN

STARRING
CARY GRANT · VICTOR McLAGLEN
DOUGLAS FAIRBANKS, Jr.

with SAM JAFFE · EDUARDO CIANNELLI · JOAN FONTAINE
PANDRO S. BERMAN, IN CHARGE OF PRODUCTION
PRODUCED AND DIRECTED BY GEORGE STEVENS
Screen play by Joel Sayre & Fred Guiol · From a story by Ben Hecht
& Charles MacArthur · Inspired by Rudyard Kipling's Poem

R K O RADIO PICTURES

WORLD PREMIERE JANUARY 26th · RADIO CITY MUSIC HALL
IN YOUR CITY SOON—Watch your newspapers for local playdates.

A TOWN...A STRANGER...

and the things he does to its people... especially its women!

CinemaScope
TECHNICOLOR

Picnic

WILLIAM HOLDEN
KIM NOVAK
AND CO-STARRING
ROSALIND RUSSELL

169

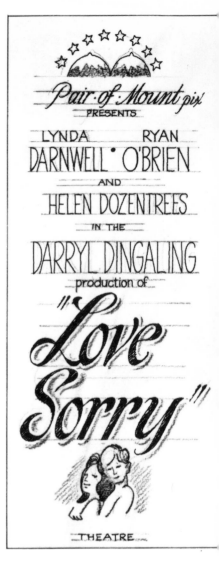

1

2

3

1. **Darryl Dingaling, Mighty Movie Mogul and Prismatic Producer,** usually gets the campaign rolling while discussing his latest production with a few of his "boys" at his local hangout. After several double extra-dry Harvey Wallbangers, he is suddenly inspired and jots his first thoughts on the bar's cocktail napkin. "Brilliant! That's it! Bartender! Another Harvey Wallbanger, please!"

2. One of the "boys" is dispatched with this very valuable piece of napkin to the agency, where he personally places it into the very hands of the President, Vice Presidents, Chairman of the Board and the Account Director. Immediately it is photostatted fifty times to insure protection in case the original napkin is—God forbid—lost. The Art Director and his layout man are given copies and proceed to work up rough layouts. (They're totally confused, of course, since they have seen neither a script nor a billing sheet nor a set of movie stills.)

3. An incomplete billing sheet arrives attached to a memo from the Desk of Darryl Dingaling complimenting them on the beauty of the first layout. However, just a few minor changes are required... reduce the clinch art by at least 75% and goose up the credits and title considerably. Otherwise, fine... and please retain the original layout look.

Evolution of a Movie Ad

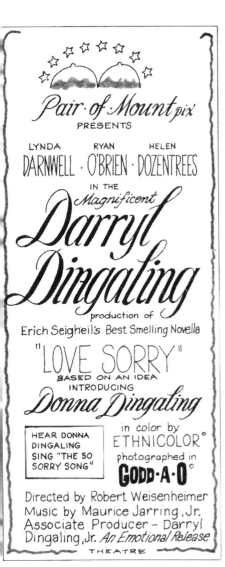

4

5

6

4. A billing sheet arrives with two stills and an incomplete script. The attached Dingaling Desk Note informs the Agency that the clinch scene has been deleted from the picture, so take out the art from the ad and make it an all-type ad, but retain the look of the original layout. The note also suggests that since there will be no clinch art, it might be wise to make Dingaling's name much stronger than the title to insure a certain drawing power at the box-office. In a letter to the Board of Directors at Pair-of-mount Studios, he suggests an added scene, and a song utilizing the outstanding talents of his wife. And if he brought in his son as Associate Producer, this film would, indeed, be a true Dingaling movie! Erich Seigheil believes his best-smelling novella and inspiration of the Dingaling Production is just as, if not more, important than Donna Dingaling, and presses his agent and lawyer to insist upon author's billing above the title.

5. No one, except Darryl and Donna Dingaling, is delirious about the ad as it finally stands. A research consultant and a media analyst are summoned and, after seven week's deliberation, report that the "Youth Market" to whom his picture is geared will (1) not see a picture without young lovers clinching or something, (2) be terribly unimpressed with star names and (3) have all read the book and eagerly await the film version. Dingaling gives in to the decision and scraps Donna and her song for a newly filmed insertion of sex scenes. The Agency gets a new, "with-it," dynamic and exciting studio to approach the problem with a "fresh mind." They, in turn, commission a famous Saturday Evening Ghost cover artist to paint a clinch and hire Arnold Toynbee to come up with a catchy copy-line.

6. The charges for the services of the Agency, the Studio, the Artist and Toynbee mount rapidly. A total fee for the work done to date is sent to the Producer for payment. One week later, Dingaling demands that everything, including type ordered, tissue paper roughs, layouts, stats and each stage of presented art be sent to his suite at the hospital. He checks everything against the itemized charges and from the bottom of a dusty large envelope marked #1, he comes across the original cocktail napkin. "But what's this!?!, he exclaims. "Brilliant! This is it! It's our Campaign! Just what I wanted from the beginning! Why didn't that jerk Agency show me this in the first place? Its got flair! Guts! Youth! Where it's at! Print it!"

by Jim Pearsall

From a Movie Ad Man's Desk

Jim Pearsall

"**W**hat's playin' at the Roxy? I'll tell you what's playin' at the Roxy—a picture about a Minnesota man so in love with a Mississippi girl that he sacrifices everything and moves all the way to Biloxi... *That's* what's playin' at the Roxy."*

Well, at least we know what's playin' at the Roxy.

Now, let's get all that into an ad so we can get moviegoers into a theatre.

Easy, you say.

O.K. *You* get out *your* drawing pad and your 6B pencil and portray a man from Minnesota, a miss from Mississippi, his everything sacrifice, his move "all the way," and the entire skyline and population of Biloxi. Consider, also, that the producer demands his ad contain an intriguing twenty-nine-word copy line in large block letters, 100% billing for the title of the picture, the leading man, the leading lady and the seventeen supporting players, 50% billing for himself, his executive producer, his associate producer, the director, the costume designer, the music composer, the writer of the screenplay, the adapter who adapted the script from a Broadway play, the playwright who wrote the Broadway play, the author of the best-selling novel on which the play was based, the Technicolor slug, the rating, the theatre's logo, the theatre's address, phone number and the feature times.

The producer expresses, also, his burning desire for a "clean" ad (one that leaves lots of white area to insure its not getting "lost" on a page with hundreds of cluttered and space-filling ads). He then informs you that since his budget is sparse, he would like the ad not to exceed thirty lines of space

(approximately 2″ x 1″). So, "enthusiastically," the advertising agency sets to work to assemble an attractive, eye-capturing, "different" kind of ad. As you take leave of the producer's or the distributor's mahogany-paneled, trophy-ridden, award-encrusted boardroom, he thrusts his last harpoon into your anticipatory breast..."O.K., guys, just let yourself go—take your time—and gimmee a commercial, sparkly, thought-provoking, deep, profound, pizazzy, class campaign...and oh, yeah, fellas, I forgot to tell you...I'll need it tomorrow nine a.m. sharp...we open the flick day after tomorrow."

Heigh-ho, heigh-ho, back to the shoe-maker's shop the little elves go. And that's one of the *easy* assignments. More often than not, production companies will demand an ad "out of the not so clear sky." No script available—they're still re-writing or they're shooting "ad lib" as they go—no stills available—the director is filming on a closed set and positively no photographers will be admitted—or he is filming on the very tippy-top of the Pyrenees and no photographers can *get* there!—no title available..."just leave a space"—they're coming up with something better than *The Beatitudes of the Buxom Beauties*—no casting or credit sheet is available—the producer is in Paris still searching for a few permissive "pastries." Nevertheless, the word is *GO*—they would like to see something by the day after tomorrow, as they expect to open with a $2,000,000.00 ad campaign two years from next Christmas and there's no sense in wasting valuable time...

Generally, the producers suggest their ad men "jot" down a few thumb-nails, roughs, and ideas—nothing elaborate, mind you—and we'll "play it by ear from there." Of course this request is greeted with suppressed gales of thrashing laughter by the agency

boys...because if, right off the bat, you don't come up with a two-by-three-foot rendering of Andrew Wyeth calibre, the producers can't possibly imagine what in blue blazes you're trying to convey and consequently charge sabotage and shoot your efforts down with the aid of their firing squad composed of wee yes-men. A producer's genius for assembling talents to make a motion picture does not necessarily match his genius for a go at the old drawing board... However, in all fairness, a total stranger does not tell a possessive mother that her "baby" would look better in pink than in puce. And the producer's product *is* his "baby"... he has labored it, born it and sweated it and no two-bit Mad Ave. punk is going to tell *him* how to design his birth announcement! But, on the other hand, the agencies and the artists can't wait around for "Big Daddy" to see what his "Baby" looks like before they release the news of the "immaculate conception." The public must know that the event occurs a week from *next* Wednesday at the Rialto—not a week ago *last* Wednesday. It's a pity there is no great award for the men and women who conjure up, design, execute, sell, promote, publicize, illustrate, photograph, retouch, set type, and slave to make it all come true. For me and most of my moom-pitcher-ad cohorts, the award is the pleasure in announcing the coming love affair, hurricane, Spring, tragedy, or bomb—all "Big Daddy's Babies." True, sometimes the announcement is "schlocky," but we are fulfilling "Big Daddy's" request... and *he's* paying the bills...and he wants *you* to know what's playin' at the Roxy...or the Strand...or the Cinema...or the Bijou...or the theatre near you...

---

*From "Guys And Dolls" by Frank Loesser

© 1950, 1951, 1953 FRANK MUSIC CORP.
Used by Permission

172

It was the
look in her eyes
that did it!

How could he resist?
How could he know it meant
MURDER?

EXPERTS BAFFLED!
Five minutes before
the close of this
suspenseful picture we
stopped the screening...
and CHALLENGED THE
LEADING MYSTERY EXPERTS
to solve the story!

Not one could give the
answer to the Greatest
Mystery Ever Filmed!

INTERNATIONAL PICTURES, INC., presents

EDWARD G. ROBINSON
and
JOAN BENNETT
with
RAYMOND MASSEY
and
Edmond Breon · Dan Duryea
RELEASED BY RKO RADIO PICTURES, INC.

"The
Woman
in the
Window"

DIRECTED BY FRITZ LANG

A NUNNALLY JOHNSON production

GOOD ENTERTAINMENT
IS INTERNATIONAL!

Brave Men...
AND THE BRAVE WOMEN WHO FOLLOW THEM!

Go with them...through the Khyber
Pass! Watch the bitter struggle between East and
West. Thrill to the love story of a brave woman
who followed her man among seething tribes. A
majestic episode in the historic drama of India.

Alexander Korda
PRESENTS

DRUMS
IN GLORIOUS TECHNICOLOR
with
SABU · RAYMOND MASSEY · DESMOND TESTER
ROGER LIVESEY · VALERIE HOBSON
And a cast of 3,000 · DIRECTED BY ZOLTAN KORDA
FROM A STORY BY A. E. W. MASON
RELEASED THRU UNITED ARTISTS
COMING SOON TO YOUR FAVORITE THEATRE—ASK THE MANAGER WHEN!

A
MOVIE QUIZ
250,000.00 CONTEST
PICTURE

Thrill to the most majestic
scenery on earth...the Hima-
layas of India...in Technicolor.

See Sabu, native Indian lad, cast
as native Indian prince, riding
triumphantly his plunging white
charger!

See real British
Troops fight where
they battled long ago
to win an Empire.

Go to the feast where dining
was only a prelude to be-
trayal...and fear rose in
the hearts of the bravest!

THE GREATNESS OF THE SCREEN...THE MAGIC OF RADIO...
COMBINED IN THE GREATEST MUSICAL OF THEM ALL!

ALICE
FAYE
JOHN
PAYNE
JACK
OAKIE

THE GREAT
AMERICAN
BROADCAST

.....From the
studio that gave
you "That Night
in Rio"!

with CESAR ROMERO
Mary Beth Hughes · James Newill
Nicholas Brothers · Wiere Brothers
The Four Ink Spots
Directed by Archie Mayo
Associate Producer Kenneth Macgowan
Original Screen Play by Don Ettlinger and
Edwin Blum, Robert Ellis and Helen Logan
A 20th CENTURY-FOX PICTURE

New HIT
SONGS
by Mack Gordon
and Harry Warren!
"LONG AGO LAST NIGHT"
"I TAKE TO YOU"
"I'VE GOT A BONE TO
PICK WITH YOU"
"THE GREAT AMERICAN
BROADCAST"
"WHERE YOU ARE"
"IT'S ALL IN A LIFETIME"

Dances staged by
Hermes Pan

Radio Ad Songs: "Chesterstrikes" · "Chapman's Cheerful Cheese" · "Porter's Puppy Biscuits" · "Wavo"

173

Gone With the Wind

Even before the first ad was published, David O. Selznick's production of *Gone with the Wind* had reaped more publicity than any other motion picture in the history of the industry. The search for an actress to portray Scarlett O'Hara was a subject of controversy. The press reported the behind-the-scenes maneuvering regarding the endless succession of actresses vying for the role of the century. The eventual selection of Vivien Leigh caused a great deal of comment because she was British. The casting of the other roles resulted in a great deal of publicity, although on a lesser scale. Clark Gable had the role of Rhett Butler tied up from the beginning—the public would accept no one else in the part.

The tremendous popularity of the novel was both advantageous and disadvantageous. Obviously there was no need to launch a campaign to introduce the film but the degree to which the general public had taken the novel and its characters to its heart provided its own set of problems. Selznick had to be sure that the film lived up to the public's expectations. He had to be sure that the actors and actresses selected would be accepted as the perfect living embodiments of Margaret Mitchell's characters.

It was not only Selznick's inherent sense of perfection and eye for detail which demanded that the film be an accurate portrayal of the South. The world was waiting for this film.

The series of ads for *Gone with the Wind* shown on this page are fascinating, for taken in sequence they reflect to a small degree the changing mores of society in general. The first ad, published in 1940, is a simple one, merely announcing that the movie was available for viewing. It assumed that the reader was familiar with the film. The ad is notable in another respect. The only part of the credits that receives any emphasis is the title. No mention is made of the story line, nor do the stars receive any play.

The second ad, for the film's reissue in 1947, is quite different. A more pedestrian approach is used and the copy line almost resembled one for a film that had faced censorship problems. (There had been a censorship problem regarding Gable's last line to Scarlett—"Frankly, my dear, I don't give a damn"—but the Hays office passed it, considering the prestigious nature of the entire project.) The classic announcement ad has been abandoned in favor of an illustration of Rhett holding Scarlett in his arms, a subtle depiction of the famous staircase scene. But despite lines like "the screen's most exciting love story and the most talked-about picture ever made," in the illustration Rhett is careful not to look at Scarlett. In the credits section of the ad, the stars are accorded more attention.

The schmeer technique is employed in the next ad, used in connection with the next re-release. The ad shows various scenes from the film including the staircase scene but it is in the background and not emphasized. An illustration of Rhett tenderly kissing Scarlett's cheek is in the foreground and is the major focus of the ad. Metro-Goldwyn-Mayer shares equal billing with Selznick.

The film was reissued again in 1961 to share in the celebration of the Civil War Centennial. The same (or similar) illustration used in the second ad is the main feature, with the addition of several scenes from the film. The scenes themselves and their captions emphasize the epic qualities of the film. This ad is also mentions the ten Academy Awards won by the movie.

The final ad in the sequence exploits the fact that the film can be seen in wide-screen, stereophonic sound and Metrocolor. For the first time Margaret Mitchell's name is not followed by the line "Story Of The Old South." The illustration of Rhett holding Scarlett has become far more sexual and they're seen looking directly into each other's eyes. Although various scenes from the movie are illustrated, this ad is far cleaner than the two preceding it. There is little claim copy and no captions are used. One point common to all the ads is the absence of critics' quotes.

SALUTING
THE CIVIL WAR
CENTENNIAL!
★★★★★★★★★★
The spectacular
romance that
thrilled millions!

DAVID O. SELZNICK'S
PRODUCTION OF
MARGARET MITCHELL'S
STORY OF THE OLD SOUTH

GONE WITH
THE WIND

Winner of Ten
Academy Awards

IN
TECHNICOLOR
STARRING
CLARK GABLE
VIVIEN LEIGH
LESLIE HOWARD
OLIVIA de HAVILLAND
A SELZNICK INTERNATIONAL PICTURE
RELEASED BY
METRO-GOLDWYN-MAYER INC.

THE GREATEST MOTION PICTURE EVER MADE!

DAVID O. SELZNICK'S Production of
MARGARET MITCHELL'S Story of the Old South
"GONE WITH THE WIND"
in TECHNICOLOR

starring CLARK GABLE · VIVIEN LEIGH
LESLIE HOWARD
OLIVIA de HAVILLAND
A SELZNICK INTERNATIONAL PICTURE
Directed by VICTOR FLEMING   Screen Play by SIDNEY HOWARD
A METRO-GOLDWYN-MAYER Masterpiece Release   MUSIC BY MAX STEINER

In new screen splendor...The most magnificent picture ever!

DAVID O. SELZNICK'S PRODUCTION OF MARGARET MITCHELL'S
"GONE WITH THE WIND"

Winner
of Ten
Academy
Awards

STARRING
CLARK GABLE
VIVIEN LEIGH
LESLIE HOWARD   OLIVIA de HAVILLAND
A SELZNICK INTERNATIONAL PICTURE · VICTOR FLEMING   SCREEN PLAY BY SIDNEY HOWARD   RE-RELEASED BY METRO-GOLDWYN-MAYER INC.   Music by MAX STEINER
IN WIDE SCREEN · STEREOPHONIC SOUND · METROCOLOR

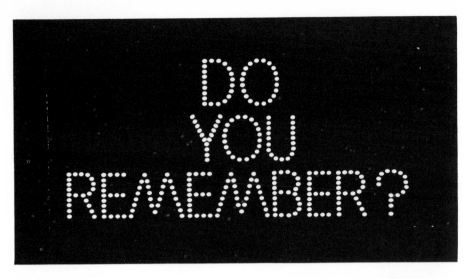

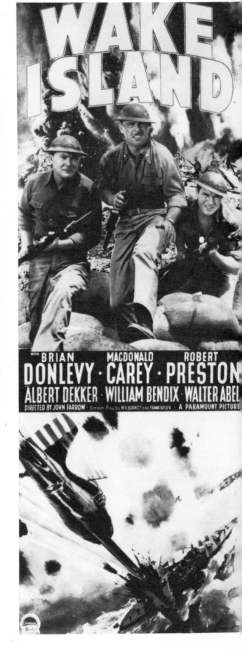

THE PICTURE DESTINED TO STARTLE THE WORLD!

KING KONG

with
FAY WRAY · ROB'T ARMSTRONG · BRUCE CABOT

A COOPER-SCHOEDSACK PRODUCTION—AN RKO RADIO PICTURE—of course!
From a Story by Edgar Wallace and Merian C. Cooper—David O. Selznick, Executive Producer

RKO RADIO PICTURES • RKO BUILDING • RADIO CITY • NEW YORK

188

Selling Technical Changes

Major technical innovations naturally warranted major space in advertising copy. The public had to be informed that this was the "first film" ever shot in this "new process!" Sound was of course of monumental importance. Less important, at least when introduced, was color. And later, in the early fifties, in an attempt to woo audiences away from TV and back into theatres, there came 3-D, CinemaScope and Stereophonic Sound.

"The Trail of the Lonesome Pine"

A new treat awaits movie fans, judging from Hollywood reports about Paramount's "The Trail of the Lonesome Pine." Sylvia Sidney, Fred MacMurray and Henry Fonda have the star roles supported by Fred Stone, Nigel Bruce, Robert Barret, Fuzzy Knight and Little Spanky McFarland. Henry Hathaway, brilliant
* Technicolor process

director of "Lives of a Bengal Lancer," has the directorial assignment. Walter Wanger pro-duces. Most interesting, is the fact that "The Trail of the Lonesome Pine" is the first full-length outdoor romantic drama to be produced in natural color*. Those who have seen it say the scenes are breath-taking in their beauty.

With the introduction of sound, movies were advertised with such
lines as "100% All Talking!" Talking pictures naturally led to musicals
and soon ads screamed: "All Talking! All Singing! All Dancing!"

Not only did people find it fascinating to hear movies talk, but they
could finally hear their favorite stars: "What does Garbo sound like?"
"Garbo Talks!"

Surprisingly, early color films were not splashily advertised as they
were in later years. The technical generic name, Technicolor, became
part of the national vocabulary.

However, with 3-D, Cinemascope, VistaVision, Panavision, etc.,
technical innovations became big selling points in ad campaigns. After
the first movies in these new processes, subsequent movies were
advertised with lines such as: "The First Crime-Of-Passion Film Shot
in Cinemascope!", etc.

Of all the technical innovations, 3-D is perhaps the most memorable.

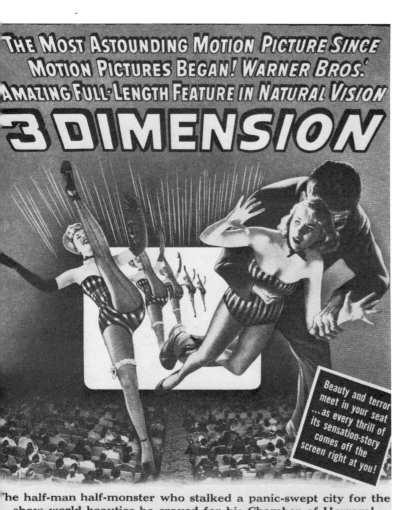

192

A motion picture event! First to be filmed in the fabulous new M-G-M Camera 65 process is the prize-winning panoramic novel "Raintree County".

M-G-M presents in M-G-M CAMERA 65

MONTGOMERY CLIFT
as Johnny Shawnessy

ELIZABETH TAYLOR
as Susanna Drake

EVA MARIE SAINT
as Nell Gaither

in

RAINTREE COUNTY

In the great tradition of Civil War Romance

However, it was too gimmicky for a long life. Soon afterwards, multi-camera Cinerama was introduced, and 3-D and the glasses necessary view it faded into oblivion. CinemaScope and stereophonic sound, however, made such an impact that almost all major films are now photographed in the wide screen process and select number of older film have been rechanneled for the new scope and sound — most notably, *Gone With The Wind.*

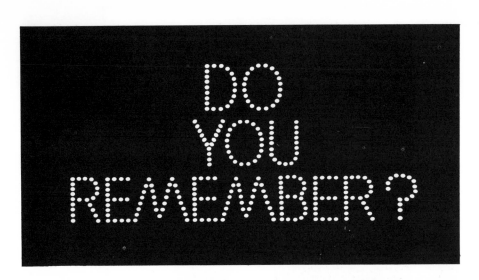

Throwaways

Little card-like leaflets, commonly known as *throwaways*, were provided in bulk (sometimes at a modest charge) to local exhibitors to be distributed as a means of promotion. Throwaways are in essence sophisticated handbills—a direct exhibitor-to-public method of selling a film.

Throwaways were handed out during promotional tours and activities. They were distributed at the theatre, as part of coming attractions, in waiting crowds, stores and anywhere else the exhibitor could arrange to have them handed out.

Often throwaways were quite creative. In addition to showing scenes from the film, they tried to capture the essence of the film and capitalize on the movie's stars. Frequently, as much care was lavished on the artwork and copy for throwaways as for the print campaign. Note the railroad ticket for *Danger Lights* and the ballot for the Ben Turpin film.

Throwaways are still in use—although they are much less popular. They are often distributed with record albums and mailing pieces.

Closed   *Open*

Open

204

Closed

Open

Closed

Open

Closed

Open

Stars

Since nickelodeon days, stars have been used to sell a movie. In the beginning, moviegoers went to see their favorite stars regardless of the film. The phenomenal boxoffice power of personalities continued throughout the 1920's, '30's and '40's. However, by the mid-1950's the mere presence of stars no longer guaranteed financial success of a film. Stars were still important, but the audience demanded more for its money than a glittering cast.

During the heyday of the stars, movie advertising generally spotlighted the particular actors by featuring their likenesses and names more prominently than the titles of the movie. Despite the fact that *Rebecca of Sunnybrook Farm* was a famous play, Mary Pickford's name was used to sell the film. The ads for *Tramp, Tramp, Tramp* were selling the star, Harry Langdon, not the movie itself.

At times an actor achieved such stardom that only one part of his name was needed for instant recognition on the part of

the audience—Chaplin, Garbo, Dietrich, Gable, Valentino, Bogart, Elvis, Brando—even Lassie and Rin-Tin-Tin.

Frequently, studios attempted—and succeeded—in creating stars through the use of advertising. The ads for *Between Two Women* ("Van Is HOT!", proclaimed MGM in giant ads for Van Johnson) and *Born Yesterday* ("Judy Holliday will be a Big Star!") illustrate this type of star build-up.

Performers like Liberace, Lawrence Tibbett, Lily Pons, and Ezio Pinza, who had achieved success in other media, were highlighted as stars from other media now making their movie debuts ("The Metropolitan Opera's Lawrence Tibbett!", etc.).

Mario Lanza's voice had become so famous by the 1950's that it received one hundred percent star billing in the 1954 film, *The Student Prince*, although Mario did not appear in the film.

The industry often attempted to capitalize on the drawing power of stars by producing films which featured AN ALL-STAR CAST!

In some cases, films were high quality dramas (*Grand Hotel, Executive Suite, Airport*) or plotless lavish musical production extravaganzas like *Ziegfeld Follies* and *Variety Girl*. The ads emphasized the number of big stars featured in the casts and not the story line.

210

I-G-M's TREMENDOUS TEN-STAR DRAMA OF LOVE AND AMBITION!

They fought like wildcats for power!

Executive Suite
by CAMERON HAWLEY

igh up in the skyscraper
auty and power clash
primitive conflict...
ere is the bold story
the lives and loves
rich men and
eir women...
sensational
reen drama that
ips you from start
finish!

M-G-M *presents the shocking novel on the screen*

EXECUTIVE SUITE

STARRING

WILLIAM HOLDEN · JUNE ALLYSON · BARBARA STANWYCK
FREDRIC MARCH · WALTER PIDGEON · SHELLEY WINTERS
PAUL DOUGLAS · LOUIS CALHERN

with DEAN JAGGER · NINA FOCH · TIM CONSIDINE · Screen Play by ERNEST LEHMAN
Based On the Novel by CAMERON HAWLEY · Directed by ROBERT WISE · Produced by JOHN HOUSEMAN · AN M-G-M PICTURE

211

AND MORE

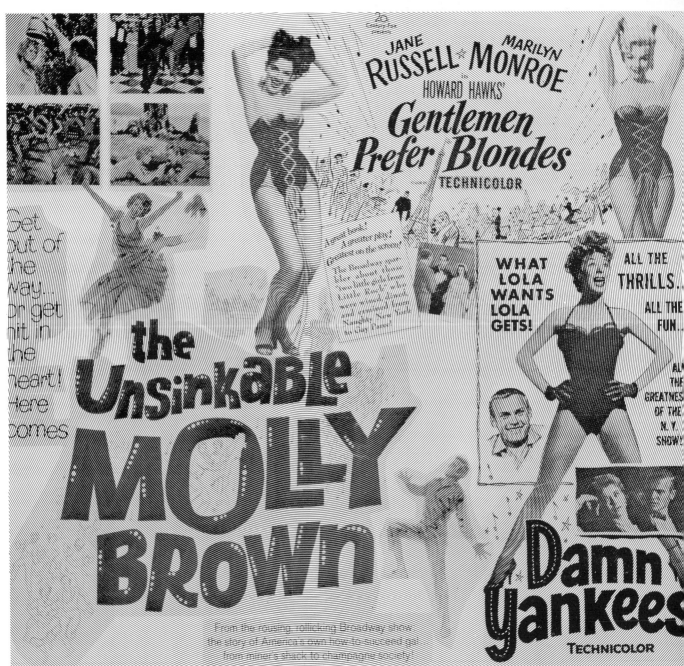

214

NIGHT FLIGHT

JOHN
BARRYMORE
HELEN HAYES
CLARK GABLE
LIONEL
BARRYMORE
ROBERT
MONTGOMERY
MYRNA LOY

A CLARENCE BROWN Production
The Spectacular Romance based on
the Prize Novel "Night Flight" has
been made into a Giant Entertainment. It takes its place alongside
of the Biggest Productions created at
the Miracle Studios of M-G-M.
David O. Selznick, Executive Producer

ONLY METRO-GOLDWYN-MAYER COULD DO IT!

The Screen's greatest star CLARA BOW

in
Gene Stratton-Porter's
Greatest Story

"The KEEPER of the BEES"

A Leo Meehan Production
Distributed by FBO Pictures Corp

TYRONE POWER

Exciting as never before . . . in the
most famous of all screen roles!

THE MARK OF Zorro

with
LINDA DARNELL
and
BASIL RATHBONE

GALE SONDERGAARD • EUGENE
PALLETTE • J. EDWARD BROMBERG
ROBERT LOWERY • CHRIS-PIN MARTIN
MONTAGU LOVE • JANET BEECHER

Associate Producer RAYMOND GRIFFITH • Directed by
ROUBEN MAMOULIAN • Screen Play by John Taintor
Foote • Adaptation by Garrett Fort • Based on the story
"The Curse of Capistrano" by Johnston McCulley
A TWENTIETH CENTURY-FOX PICTURE

A masked adventurer . . .
the jagged mark of his
sword striking terror
into every heart but hers!

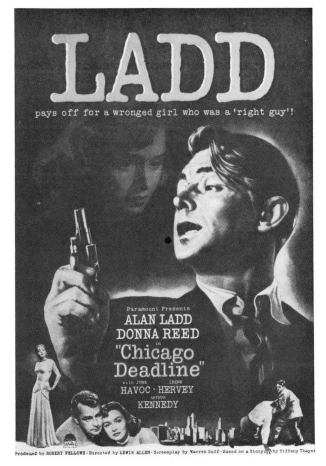

LADD

pays off for a wronged girl who was a 'right guy'!

Paramount Presents
ALAN LADD
DONNA REED
in
"Chicago Deadline"

with JUNE IRENE
HAVOC • HERVEY
ARTHUR
KENNEDY

Produced by ROBERT FELLOWS • Directed by LEWIS ALLEN • Screenplay by Warren Duff • Based on a Story by Tiffany Thayer

215

Gary Cooper

Ingrid Bergman

HE'S "WHITE HAT" THE GAMBLER

SHE'S HIS "CLIO" OF NEW ORLEANS

YOU CAN'T DREAM OF A TEAM MORE EXCITING THAN THE LOVERS IN

"SARATOGA TRUNK"

WARNERS' Biggest!

EDNA FERBER'S STORY OF STORIES • WITH FLORA ROBSON • HAL B. WALLIS PROD'N • DIRECTED BY SAM WOOD

Screenplay by Casey Robinson • Music by Max Steiner

OPENING TOMORROW

Adolph Zukor and Jesse L.Lasky present

with
BEBE DANIELS
Lois Wilson
Doris Kenyon
Lowell Sherman

RUDOLPH VALENTINO
in "Monsieur Beaucaire

a Paramount Picture

A SIDNEY OLCOTT PRODUCTION

His return to the screen after two years. The most brilliant achievement of his career! During the engagement the show will start daily at 1 P. M. Following performance start at 3-5-7 and 9.

Prices: Matinee—Children, 25c; Adults, 50c
Nights—Children, 50c; Adults, 75c; Loge, 85c

THANK YOUR STARS . . . for the Most Exciting Romantic Hit of the Whole Year!

BEAUTIFUL JOAN IN HER MOST thrilling love-drama . . . with Robert Young (I Met Him In Paris) and Franchot Tone in its brilliant cast! Life had cheated this cabaret singer of romance . . . and then she got her one big chance for happiness . . . marked "For 2 weeks only!" Your heart will tell you it's great!

JOAN Crawford in

THE BRIDE WORE RED

FRANCHOT TONE
ROBERT YOUNG

BILLIE BURKE · REGINALD OWEN
A Metro-Goldwyn-Mayer Picture

Directed by Dorothy Arzner

Produced by Joseph T

M-G-M SHORT   THEATRE

Marlene Dietrich
in
"THE SCARLET EMPRESS"
(Based on a private diary of Catherine the Great)
directed by JOSEF VON STERNBERG
A PARAMOUNT PICTURE

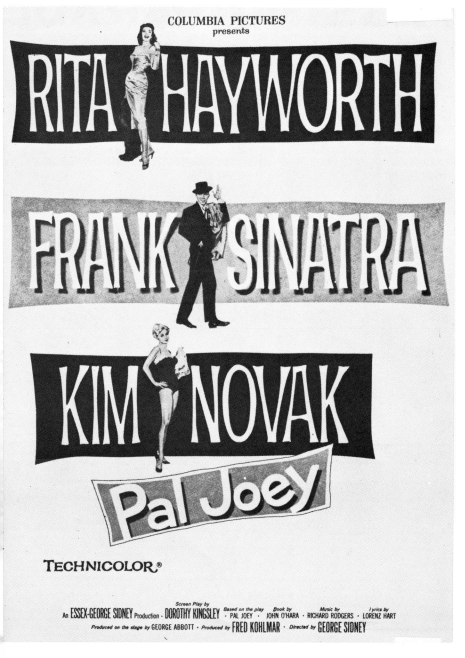

"Go See it," Says Your Favorite Star

A popular way of advertising films in the 1930's and '40's was to utilize *celebrity quotes*. In those days, when individual film critics were not nationally influential, a quote from *The New York Times* meant little to a Portland or Des Moines audience. Thus, when a studio had a film that needed prestige, or one they felt would be met with unanimous critical pans, they would screen the film for celebrities and syndicated columnists, gather the favorable

omments and use them in national ads—" 'It's The Greatest!'
ays Walter Winchell." If Rita Hayworth was capable of
onvincing millions of women to use soap, why not utilize
er to sell one of her studio's movies?

The practice faded with the emergence of powerful,
ationally known film critics and the demise of studio contract
tars. But every now and then a company will revive the
ractice. Note the campaign for *Marty*.

Tie-Ins And Endorsements

Consumer advertisers have always recognized the advantages of having certain products and services associated with a film, a star or the industry in general. All the glamour of Hollywood would be associated with a particular brand of soap if it was the soap of the st[...] Through the 1920's, '30's and '40's this type of advertising had to be handled very carefully. There was an ambivalence here because stars were "on pedestals"—they lived in a fantasy-land but at the same time had to be part of the real world.

The studios and the ad men were careful to preserve stars' aura of glamour and subtle promotion rather than hard-sell was use[...] Stars with beautiful complexions would endorse soap or beauty cream, thus implying that their beauty resulted from the product rather than nature. Sometimes sells were more direct, with personalities calling a particular brand "the best." Of course, the star's latest film was always plugged in the ad copy.

In addition, films often would have promotional tie-ups with products used in the film (airlines, buslines, food). If, for example, an airline provided a film company with free travel, in return the airline was shown on-screen in the movie. Furthermore, a cooperative advertising deal might be arranged whereby the airline's ads would carry a tag line for the film.

Promotional tie-ups can be more direct. Often a film will tie up with a specific product or line of products (the *Gigi* line of clothes for children). The film derives additional ad space off-the-movie-page and the product benefits from identification with a movie. (In addition, advertising rates on merchandising pages are much cheaper than on movie pages.)

AND MORE

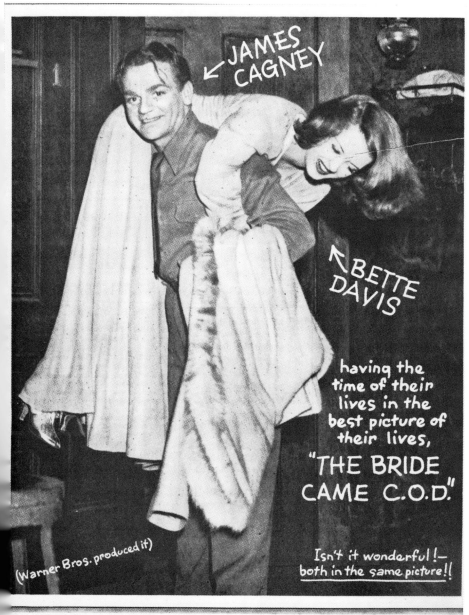

And More

And More

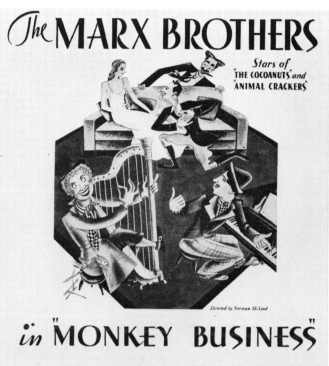

The MARX BROTHERS

Stars of
"THE COCOANUTS" and
"ANIMAL CRACKERS"

Directed by Norman McLeod

in "MONKEY BUSINESS"

*Celebrate Paramount's
20th Birthday Jubilee!*

Paramount is celebrating 20 years of leadership with the greatest pictures in its history! Watch for "24 Hours," "A Farewell to Arms," "No One Man," "Lives of a Bengal Lancer" And such stars as Harold Lloyd, George Bancroft, Marlene Dietrich, Ruth Chatterton and others in the greatest pictures of their careers!

LAUGHING days are here again! With that famous frenzied foursome, The Marx Brothers, in a new madhouse of merriment—"MONKEY BUSINESS." It's the first of the great pictures in Paramount Jubilee Month — September — when leading theatres everywhere will feature Paramount Pictures. Watch for announcements. *"If it's a Paramount Picture it's the best show in town!"*

Paramount Pictures

PARAMOUNT PUBLIX CORPORATION
ADOLPH ZUKOR, PRES. PARAMOUNT BLDG., N.Y.

Marilyn Monroe and "Niagara" a raging torrent of emotion that even nature can't control!

20th CENTURY-FOX presents "Niagara"

starring
MARILYN MONROE · JOSEPH COTTEN · JEAN PETERS · Technicolor

with CASEY ADAMS · DENIS O'DEA · RICHARD ALLAN · DON WILSON · LURENE TUTTLE · RUSSELL COLLINS · WILL WRIGHT
Produced by CHARLES BRACKETT   Directed by HENRY HATHAWAY   Written by CHARLES BRACKETT, WALTER REISCH and RICHARD BREEN

THE PICTURE EVERY WOMAN WILL WANT SOME MAN TO SEE

If you know of anything more important than the female of the species in the world's scheme of things, then you can dispute our action in awarding this new Kay Francis picture runaway honors as the outstanding photoplay of the month. See it and you will know why woman critics unite in calling it the greatest picture of its kind since "Stella Dallas"—even greater, perhaps, because of its modern viewpoint and open honesty in considering a love problem women in the day of "Stella Dallas" kept padlocked in their hearts. The role of a mother, caught in the turmoil of a love so desperate that she must break another woman's heart or her own, is valiantly performed by

KAY FRANCIS
IN
"GIVE ME YOUR HEART"

From a Noted Stage Play . . . With

GEORGE BRENT

Roland Young • • Patric Knowles
Henry Stephenson • Frieda Inescort
Directed by Archie L. Mayo • A Cosmopolitan Production

THE PICTURE OF THE MONTH

Only to a world of advancing social ideas would the screen dare present so fearlessly candid a drama. And only for a public whose tastes have been keyed to a higher entertainment level could Warner Bros. have included it in that remarkable succession of new-season pictures which has already given us "The Green Pastures" and "Anthony Adverse." A happy movie season is indeed in store for us with assurance from trustworthy sources that Warner Bros. have issued confidential orders that the same standard of excellence be adhered to in the production of Marion Davies and Clark Gable's "Cain and Mabel"; "Charge of the Light Brigade," with Errol Flynn and Olivia de Havilland; Lloyd C. Douglas' celebrated best-seller, "Green Light," and other forthcoming pictures.

IMAGINE!
They're all in one picture and it's a sensation!

CLARK GABLE
SPENCER TRACY
CLAUDETTE COLBERT
HEDY LAMARR
in
BOOM TOWN

Screen Play by John Lee Mahin • Based on a Story by James Edward Grant • Directed by
JACK CONWAY • Produced by Sam Zimbalist • *A METRO-GOLDWYN-MAYER PICTURE*

ROY SINGS THE ANSWER TO A GYPSY LOVE CALL!

It's a carnival of romantic musical thrills when a wild-ridin' cowboy crosses trails with a wild-lovin' gypsy.

Meet ESTELITA RODRIGUEZ, The Gypsy Bombshell! She's Sensational!

Hear ROY Sing this No.1 Song Hit "ALONG THE NAVAJO TRAIL" to Dale Evans!

Roy Rogers · Trigger
KING OF THE COWBOYS
THE SMARTEST HORSE IN THE MOVIES
IN
ALONG THE NAVAJO TRAIL

Featuring GEORGE "GABBY" HAYES and DALE EVANS
with ESTELITA RODRIGUEZ and DOUGLAS FOWLEY · NESTOR PAIVA and
BOB NOLAN and THE SONS OF THE PIONEERS · A REPUBLIC PICTURE

Your eyes
will open wide with wonder!

The picture you dreamed some day
you'd see . . . lovely to look at, lovelier
still as you listen! A musical romance
gay and magnificent, skimming in shim-
mering delight along the silvery Alpine
slopes! Spectacle so splendid, beauty
so breath-taking that it's all you've ever
longed for in entertainment . . . as your
"One In A Million" girl finds the boy
in a million!

SONJA · TYRONE
HENIE · POWER

Thin Ice

A PLEASURE TO HEAR!
"My Secret Love Affair"
"Over Night"
"My Swiss Hilly Billy"
By Pollack and Mitchell
"I'm Olga from the Volga"
By Gordon & Revel

ARTHUR TREACHER
RAYMOND WALBURN
JOAN DAVIS
SIG RUMANN · ALAN HALE
LEAH RAY · MELVILLE COOPER
MAURICE CASS · GEORGE GIVOT
Directed by Sidney Lanfield
. . . who gave you "Sing, Baby, Sing",
"One In A Million", "Wake Up And Live"
Associate Producer Raymond Griffith
Screen Play by Boris Ingster and Milton Sperling
From the play "Der Komet" by Attila Orbok
DARRYL F. ZANUCK in Charge of Production

20th CENTURY FOX
Your guarantee of the best
in entertainment!

Zola —the rebel genius life never tamed—strides
across the screen to become an immortal character in the motion picture gallery of the great!

The outstanding prestige picture of
the season. —Time

The most distinguished and most
important contribution to the
screen this year.
—Kate Cameron, N Y Daily News

The finest historical film ever made
and the greatest screen biography.
—Frank Nugent, N Y Times

So far superior . . . no superlative
that this department temporarily
abandoned its job of being critical
—The Digest

Warner Bros. proudly present

Mr. Paul MUNI in THE LIFE OF EMILE ZOLA

WITH A CAST OF THOUSANDS INCLUDING:
Gale Sondergaard . . . . Joseph Schildkraut
Gloria Holden · Donald Crisp · Erin O'Brien-Moore ·
Henry O'Neill · Louis Calhern · Morris Carnovsky · Directed
by William Dieterle Screen play by Norman Reilly Raine, Heinz Herald and Geza Herczeg

Soon to be shown
at popular prices!

Don't miss the picture that packed America's leading theatres for
weeks at $2.20 a seat. Coming to your favorite theatre soon.

And More

Films From Other Lands

Advertising for foreign movies is significant because some of the techniques employed eventually were adopted by the entire industry.

Ads for foreign films are usually characterized by an abundance of white space. There is seldom any claim copy and the artwork is usually classically simple.

Logos and subtle pen and ink sketches are ordinarily the predominant types of art work used. A "schmeer" approach is sometimes put into effect after the film has bombed or it leaves first run and goes on showcase.

Critics quotes have always played a major role in ads for foreign films. In the early stages of the Foreign Film Movement, a rave review from a nationally known newspaper or magazine critic gave an imported movie a high degree of respectability and acceptance with the general public. The success of *And God Created Woman,* the first Brigitte Bardot movie to achieve wide popularity in the U.S., can be largely attributed to the exposure given the favorable reviews published by *Life, The New York Times* and *The New York Daily News.* That campaign also resisted the temptation to exploit the obvious sexual implications of the film, its star and its title.

The purity of the ad for Jean Renoir's *Grand Illusion,* reissued in the late 1950's, illustrates the intellectual approach to advertising. The title is the focal point and the stars' names are given virtually no emphasis. The citation by the Brussels Film Festival followed by a minimum of claim copy represents a good example of the subtle soft sell.

Despite the sensational copy used in the ads for *La Dolce Vita,* the concept remained the same. The title received all the emphasis. The photograph of Anita Ekberg holding a kitten eventually became synonymous with the film.

Films from Other Lands

Pressbooks for foreign movies usually offered exhibitors two approaches to selling the films. Artistic ads for the original language version were usually emphasized in urban centers. The alternate approach ads for the English language version were more flamboyant and usually emphasized the sensational aspects of the film.

In recent years, foreign directors have garnered *auteur* followings and the advertising has used directors' names to sell films. Foreign films have led the way in deemphasizing the stars and emphasizing the director.

"**The last word in thrillers. Terrific.**"
—Gene Shalit, Look Magazine

"**Enough intrigue and excitement to eclipse James Bond.**"
—Playboy

"**'Z' damn, near knocks you out of your seat.**"
—Pauline Kael, The New Yorker

"**An 'A' for 'Z'. Stands without peer as a document and thriller.**"
—Judith Crist, NBC-TV

YVES MONTAND   IRENE PAPAS   JEAN-LOUIS TRINTIGNANT

Z

GP

Academy Award Nomination · Best Picture of the Year

The Great Suspense Film That Shocked the World... And Became A Classic.

Henri-Georges Clouzot's

DIABOLIQUE

starring SIMONE SIGNORET · VERA CLOUZOT
A SEVEN ARTS PICTURES RELEASE

A Carlo Ponti Production

Michelangelo Antonioni's

BLOW-UP

Vanessa Redgrave
David Hemmings
Sarah Miles

A Premier Productions Co., Inc. Release

COLOR

Special Situations

Lana Turner's private life was the source of the copywriter's inspiration for the adlines of *Another Time, Another Place*. The film was rushed into release immediately following the Turner-Johnny Stompanato scandal.

Milton Berle, who never made it as a star in films in the 1930's and '40's, returned to the medium a full-fledged superstar after his phenomenal success on TV. Note, however, that the ad for *Always Leave Them Laughing* never mentions TV, a *verboten* subject at the time to Warner Brothers studio chief Jack L. Warner

Boeing Boeing is one example of contractual billing reaching ridiculous proportions—who gets top billing ?

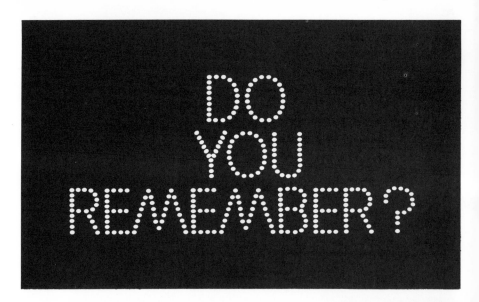

BLONDE BOMBER

...(America's newest glamour girl, VERONICA LAKE) raids the hearts of four flying aces...

Paramount Producer ARTHUR HORNBLOW, Jr. and Paramount Director MITCHELL LEISEN who created "Arise, My Love," set this daring story of tangled loves against the roaring background of America's great flying legion to give you the biggest and the best of all air pictures.

"I WANTED WINGS"

starring

RAY MILLAND · WILLIAM HOLDEN · WAYNE MORRIS · BRIAN DONLEVY

with CONSTANCE MOORE · VERONICA LAKE · HARRY DAVENPORT

Directed by MITCHELL LEISEN · A Paramount Picture

ASK YOUR THEATRE MANAGER WHEN THIS BIG PARAMOUNT HIT IS COMING

20th CENTURY-FOX HAS MADE THE GREATEST MUSICAL EXTRAVAGANZA EVER BROUGHT TO THE SCREEN!

in TECHNICOLOR!

DOWN ARGENTINE WAY

with DON AMECHE · BETTY GRABLE · CARMEN MIRANDA

and CHARLOTTE GREENWOOD · J. CARROL NAISH · HENRY STEPHENSON · KATHARINE ALDRIDGE · LEONID KINSKEY · CHRIS-PIN MARTIN

Produced by Darryl F. Zanuck
Associate Producer Harry Joe Brown · Directed by Irving Cummings · Screen Play by Darrell Ware and Karl Tunberg · Story by Rian James and Ralph Spence

Music and Lyrics: "Two Dreams Met", "Down Argentine Way" (Argentina), "Nenita", "Sing To Your Senorita" by Mack Gordon and Harry Warren

Songs Sung by Carmen Miranda: "South American Way", "Bambu", "Mamae Eu Quero", "Touradas Em Madrid"

The irresistible rhythms of Rhumbas and Congas! The glamorous spell of the Argentine! A cast of stars brilliant as the Southern Cross! Show - stopping new personalities! Romance — the South American way! The spectacular entertainment two continents have been waiting for!

HOLD YOUR SEATS FOR THRILLS THAT'LL CHILL YOU...
HOLD YOUR SIDES FOR LAUGHS THAT'LL KILL YOU...

EDDIE BRACKEN VERONICA LAKE

"HOLD THAT BLONDE"

FOR LOVE THAT'LL FILL YOU FULL OF JOY!

with ALBERT DEKKER and WILLIE BEST
Produced by Paul Jones
Directed by George Marshall
A Paramount Picture

He's got a Kleptomania for beautiful blondes, and when his ears twitch his fingers itch — from then on nothing is safe in the merriest comedy you've ever seen!

Veronica's got what it takes, so Bracken took it till she turned the tables with some taking ways of her own!

There was temptation in her helpless silence

...and then torment

WHEREVER motion pictures are shown "Johnny Belinda" will be the most discussed drama this year...
Never has the screen been more fearlessly outspoken. Rarely, if ever, has there been a story of a young girl's betrayal to touch you as will this one. You certainly will want to see it — we urge you to watch for the opening date.

WARNER BROS.
present a daring and courageous new dramatic achievement

JANE WYMAN · LEW AYRES

With this performance Jane Wyman unquestionably establishes her talent as among the very foremost on the screen.

The doctor first to find her secret, first to share her shame.

"Johnny Belinda"

with CHARLES BICKFORD   AGNES MOOREHEAD · STEPHEN McNALLY
DIRECTED BY JEAN NEGULESCO   PRODUCED BY JERRY WALD

THIS IS THE MATCHLESS ADVENTURE THAT SETS A NEW EXCITEMENT-PEAK FOR THE SCREEN!

ERROL FLYNN

in the thrill-swept story of 'The Robin Hood of the Seas'

The Sea Hawk

A New WARNER BROS. Success
With More than a Thousand Players, including
BRENDA MARSHALL
CLAUDE RAINS
DONALD CRISP · FLORA ROBSON
ALAN HALE
Directed by MICHAEL CURTIZ
Screen Play by Howard Koch and Seton I. Miller
Music by Erich Wolfgang Korngold
A Warner Bros.-First National Picture

Your theatre manager will tell you gladly the date of this engagement

It's Bigger AND BETTER THAN "SUN VALLEY SERENADE" BECAUSE IT'S GOT UNCLE SAM'S FIGHTING NEPHEWS...THE U.S. MARINES!

Sonja HENIE
John PAYNE

in ICELAND

with JACK OAKIE

SAMMY KAYE AND HIS ORCHESTRA

20th CENTURY-FOX

Coming in 1949

JOAN OF ARC

starring INGRID BERGMAN

COLOR BY TECHNICOLOR

than 'Sweetie'

Nancy Carroll in 'Honey'

WITH
HARRY GREEN, LILLIAN ROTH
SKEETS GALLAGHER, STANLEY SMITH

a Paramount Picture

THE GREAT "LADY EVE" COMBINATION!

BARBARA STANWYCK · HENRY FONDA

WESLEY RUGGLES' You Belong To Me

EDGAR BUCHANAN
ROGER CLARK · RUTH DONNELLY · MELVILLE COOPER
Screen play by Claude Binyon
Directed by WESLEY RUGGLES

FROM M·G·M's HALL OF FAME

THEY CALLED HER A SCARFACED SHE-DEVIL!

JOAN CRAWFORD

in her most EXCITING hit!

A Woman's Face

M-G-M'S ALL-TIME GREAT

"WHATEVER I AM, MEN MADE ME"

with MELVYN DOUGLAS

Screen Play by DONALD OGDEN STEWART and ELLIOT PAUL
Directed by GEORGE CUKOR · Produced by VICTOR SAVILLE
A METRO-GOLDWYN-MAYER PICTURE

She goes "Wolfie"...to show him the kind of Kissing he's Missing!

...so for every blonde he fondled—she went out and found 6 feet of man...

Oh, Man!

UNIVERSAL presents

George BRENT
Lucille BALL
Vera ZORINA

in Lover Come Back

A FESSIER-PAGANO PRODUCTION

with CHARLES WINNINGER

CARL ESMOND · RAYMOND WALBURN · ELISABETH RISDON
LOUISE BEAVERS · WALLACE FORD · FRANKLIN PANGBORN

Original Screenplay Written and Produced by Michael Fessier and Ernest Pagano
Directed by WILLIAM A. SEITER · Executive Producer: HOWARD BENEDICT · A UNIVERSAL PICTURE

YOUR DREAM OF PERFECT BEAUTY COMES TRUE!

Surpassing even their amazing "42nd Street," Warner Bros. now bring you the magnificent climax of screen grandeur! See "The Stairway to the Stars" and 6 other vast spectacle scenes! Learn 5 new song hits! Thrill to a fun-filled story!

Classics

As with advertising films based on successes in other media (books, plays, radio series), the film industry had a sure-fire advertising advantage when producers provided film versions of well known classics.

The campaigns for the classics were usually simple and in good taste, the ads often were designed for intellectual appeal. Occasionally, schmeer campaigns were used when the "class" campaign failed or the film moved from its first run theater into the neighborhood chain. Some epics naturally lent themselves to schmeer campaigns.

"Never has Hamlet been rendered with more clarity or more biting timeliness!

In these more than 3½ centuries there have not been more than a dozen great Hamlets. Everyone who is alive today has the rare and illuminating privilege of seeing one of them—Nicol Williamson. Never has Hamlet been rendered with more clarity or more biting timeliness, and that includes Gielgud, Olivier and Burton." —TIME

COLUMBIA PICTURES AND FILMWAYS PRESENT
A WOODFALL FILM

NICOL WILLIAMSON
HAMLET

co-starring MARIANNE FAITHFULL as Ophelia

Executive Producers
MARTIN RANSOHOFF and LESLIE LINDER
Produced by NEIL HARTLEY
Directed by TONY RICHARDSON COLOR

The motion picture of all time... for all time!...WINNER OF 5 ACADEMY AWARDS!

FOUR DAYS ONLY!

Laurence Olivier
PRESENTS
Hamlet

by WILLIAM SHAKESPEARE
A Universal-International Release
A J. ARTHUR RANK ENTERPRISE

EXCLUSIVE ENGAGEMENT
Continuous Performances
See it from the beginning
Feature starts at
12:00, 3:00, 6:00, 9:00 p.m.
Matinees: 90¢, Evenings: $1.20
Students 74¢ at all times

NORMA SHEARER · LESLIE HOWARD
in
"Romeo and Juliet"
with
JOHN BARRYMORE

EDNA MAY OLIVER · BASIL RATHBONE · C. AUBREY SMITH
ANDY DEVINE · RALPH FORBES · REGINALD DENNY · CONWAY
TEARLE · ROBERT WARWICK · VIOLET KEMBLE-COOPER

You've heard about it for months! You've read about it everywhere! It's all true. This is the greatest love drama, the mightiest entertainment of our time. Every moment throbs as sparks fly, as steel meets steel... and the crimson follows the rapier's thrust...Lovers meet ...and dream...and plan. Pomp and grandeur sweep by in spectacular pageantry. Here are thrills, suspense to spur the pulse...tender romance to charm the heart...beauty to fill the eye. A love story deep in the heart of the world forever, now given enthralling life in such a picture as the screen has never known.

*A Metro-Goldwyn-Mayer Triumph
Directed by George Cukor*

"DAZZLING! Once you see it, you'll never again picture 'Romeo & Juliet' quite the way you did before!" —LIFE

PARAMOUNT PICTURES presents
A BHE FILM
The
FRANCO ZEFFIRELLI
Production of
ROMEO & JULIET

No ordinary love story....

THE FRANCO ZEFFIRELLI PRODUCTION OF
WILLIAM SHAKESPEARE'S "ROMEO & JULIET" STARRING OLIVIA HUSSEY / LEONARD WHITING / MILO O'SHEA / MICHAEL YORK /
JOHN McENERY / PAT HEYWOOD / NATASHA PARRY / ROBERT STEPHENS /
SCREENPLAY BY FRANCO BRUSATI and MASOLINO D'AMICO / ANTHONY HAVELOCK-ALLAN and JOHN BRABOURNE
ASSOCIATE PRODUCER RICHARD GOODWIN / DIRECTED BY FRANCO ZEFFIRELLI / TECHNICOLOR® A PARAMOUNT PICTURE

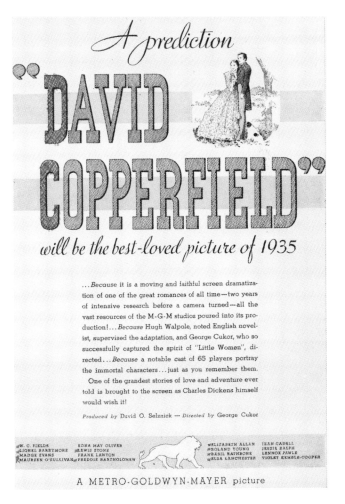

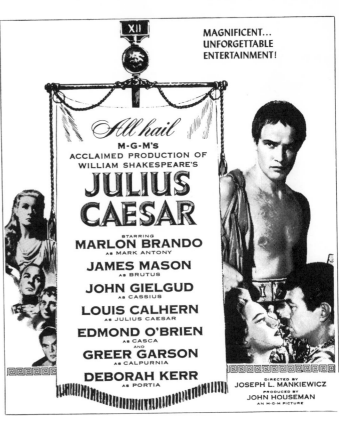

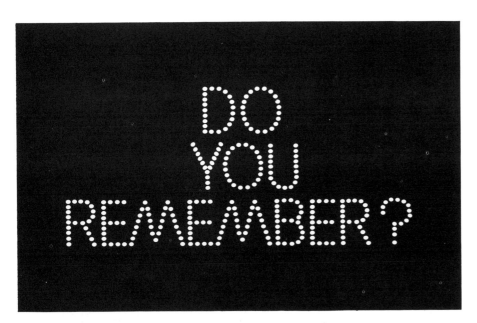

"I didn't think I'd be true to a man again as long as I lived...

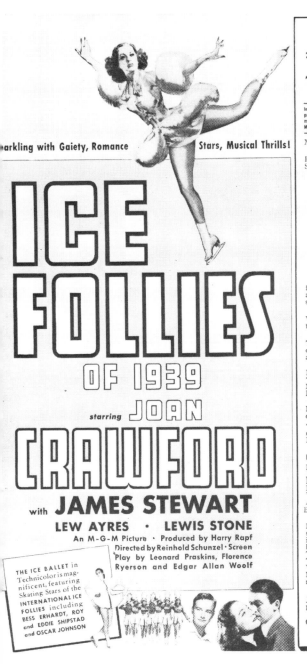

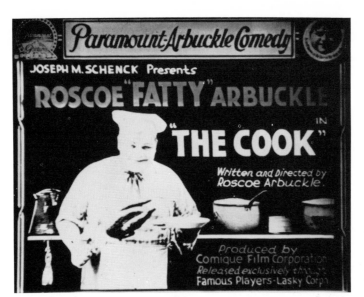

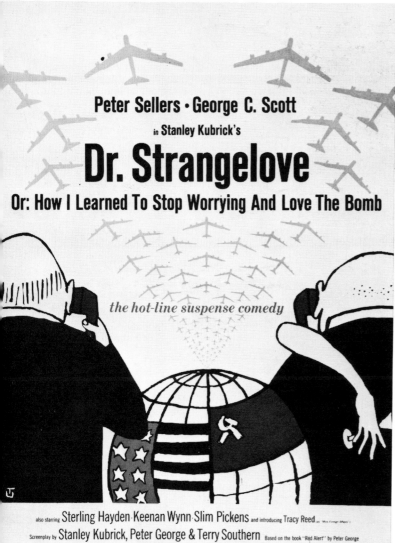

She's back (and will you ever forget her in "Broadway Melody of 1936") in the Biggest Musical Show of this Year...M-G-M's dazzling successor to "Great Ziegfeld" ...brim-full of brilliant scenes, thrilling dances, gorgeous girls, and stars — stars —STARS! The Cole Porter songs are swell ("Easy to Love", "I've Got You Under My Skin", "Swingin' The Jinx Away", "Hey, Babe, Hey", and lots more).

BORN TO DANCE
Starring ELEANOR POWELL

JAMES STEWART · VIRGINIA BRUCE
UNA MERKEL · SID SILVERS · FRANCES LANGFORD
RAYMOND WALBURN · ALAN DINEHART · BUDDY EBSEN
A Metro-Goldwyn-Mayer Picture · Directed by Roy Del Ruth

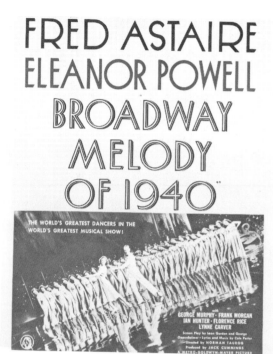

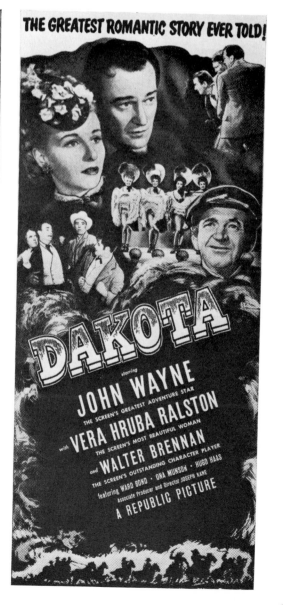

Censorship and Advertising

With the release of *The Outlaw* in 1946, producer Howard Hughes took advantage of censorship problems encountered by the film by emphasizing them in national ads.

However, *The Moon Is Blue*, released in 1953, made no direct mention that the film had problems with the censors and was being released with a seal. The ad line—*"The Picture Everyone Is Talking About"*—could refer to the lack of a seal, or to the fact that the Catholic Church had denounced the film, but it also could refer to the point that the hit play had also been highly controversial.

In later years, ads, especially those which had explicit artwork and copy or explicit titles, began encountering censorship. The ads for *Succubus* (1969) illustrates how the ad men tried to circumvent local censorship and pressures. The pressbook included several ads which had the title of the film. However, additionals ads were provided without the film's title for those newspapers which would not run the ad because they deemed the title too suggestive and erotic.

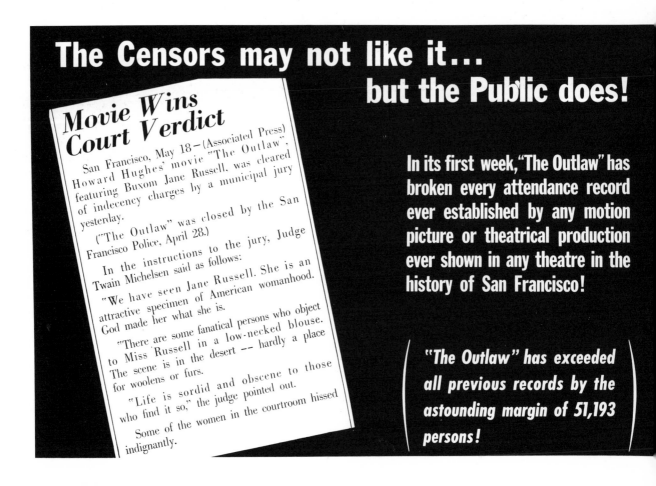

The Censors may not like it... but the Public does!

Movie Wins Court Verdict

San Francisco, May 18 – (Associated Press) Howard Hughes' movie "The Outlaw", featuring Buxom Jane Russell, was cleared of indecency charges by a municipal jury yesterday.

("The Outlaw" was closed by the San Francisco Police, April 28.)

In the instructions to the jury, Judge Twain Michelsen said as follows:

"We have seen Jane Russell. She is an attractive specimen of American womanhood. God made her what she is.

"There are some fanatical persons who object to Miss Russell in a low-necked blouse. The scene is in the desert -- hardly a place for woolens or furs.

"Life is sordid and obscene to those who find it so," the judge pointed out.

Some of the women in the courtroom hissed indignantly.

In its first week, "The Outlaw" has broken every attendance record ever established by any motion picture or theatrical production ever shown in any theatre in the history of San Francisco!

"The Outlaw" has exceeded all previous records by the astounding margin of 51,193 persons!

Let's Make It Again

Throughout its history, the motion picture industry has capitalized on past hits by reworking old scripts, changing the original setting and producing what might be called quasi-remakes. In such instances, new titles are always used as the audience is not expected to realize that the plot has been used before. This practice reached a peak during the 1930's and '40's. 20th Century-Fox, for example, remade its 1943 Betty Grable hit, *Coney Island,* seven years later, entitling it *Wabash Avenue.* Grable also starred in the remake, and there were slight changes in the script, including

a switch in locale. MGM used plot elements from its 1929 blockbuster, *Broadway Melody*, in many of its later musicals, including *Two Girls on Broadway* and *Singin' in the Rain*.

Warner Brothers was particularly famous for reworking scripts and draining the last drop from a story that had proven profitable. Paramount, in the early 1950's, reworked many old scripts for its hot comedy team of Dean Martin and Jerry Lewis. The stories were up-dated and the plots adapted for the two-man comedy team.

One some occasions, changes in scripts and locales were made to reflect new sociological trends. Paramount's 1969 release, *Up-tight,* was an adaptation of the 1935 classic, *The Informer*. The setting was changed from Ireland to Harlem and the new cast was all black. Universal's *The Lost Man* was a quasi-remake, with

idney Poitier, of the 1949 James Mason thriller, *Odd Man Out.*

Direct remakes of films must not be confused with these uasi-remakes involving reworked and retitled scripts. Direct emakes usually utilized the original title and, almost always, he original dialogue, up-dating it here and there.

The major reason for remaking a movie has usually been echnical advances. *Blood and Sand,* the 1922 Rudolph Valentino hit, vas remade twenty years later with Tyrone Power. The Power ersion, of course, was a "talkie," and in Technicolor. *Little Women,* David O. Selznick's 1935 production with Katharine Hepburn, vas remade in color in 1949 with June Allyson and Elizabeth Taylor. Vith remakes, the producer hopes to entice two potential segments f the vast audience—those who saw and liked the old movie but vho are curious about the new stars plus Technicolor and other

Cary, Katharine and Jimmy
are three jolly chums from P·H·I·L·A·D·E·L·P·H·I·A

A blue-blooded heiress (spirited, sporting, scandalizing) gets herself engaged to a self-made stuffed shirt (pompous, petty and prudish)! When she sets out to deflate him, the feathers fly! You'll love the way Katharine Hepburn bowls him over.

Besides the stuffed shirt, there are two other fellows—they both think Katharine is rare, reckless and racy. Cary Grant is the ex-husband who's crazy about removing the 'ex' and Jimmy Stewart is a reporter who hates his assignment but loves the subject of it!

Champagne flows...moonlight beams...and things look pretty romantic to Katharine and Jimmy around midnight! They look pretty suspicious to a couple of other fellows but the whole scene will be a laughing matter to you!

It's anyone's guess who's going to meet Katharine and the parson at the finish line! But it's a fast and racy story to the amazing end! (No wonder the play rocked and shocked Broadway for a solid year.)

Cary *Katharine* *James*
GRANT HEPBURN STEWART
in
The **Philadelphia Story**
with RUTH HUSSEY

JOHN HOWARD · ROLAND YOUNG · JOHN HALLIDAY · MARY NASH · VIRGINIA WEIDLER
Screen Play by Donald Ogden Stewart · Based on the Play by Philip Barry
Produced by The Theatre Guild Inc. · A Metro-Goldwyn-Mayer Picture
Directed by GEORGE CUKOR · Produced by JOSEPH L. MANKIEWICZ

technical advancements, and those who never saw the film in its original version, but have heard of it.

Dramas are often remade as musicals. The hit play and subsequent movie, *Philadelphia Story,* was redone as the musical *High Society. A Star Is Born,* the 1937 David O. Selznick production, was remade as a vehicle for Judy Garland in 1954.

Frequently, a film is remade solely for the purpose of up-dating. The new version reflects the latest trends in fashion, automobiles, speech patterns, etc. *Back Street,* which was remade three times, *Imitation of Life* twice and *Young at Heart,* a musical remake of *Four Daughters,* are typical of this practice.

More than once, a remake has turned out to be more dated than its prototype. *The Opposite Sex,* MGM's 1955 remake of its 1938 blockbuster *The Women,* is a case in point.

There are very rare cases when films, usually period pieces like *Gone with the Wind, Sound of Music* and Cecil B. DeMille's 1956 production of *The Ten Commandments,* will never be dated in their costuming, settings, etc. These are reissued rather than remade, since they were superbly done, and major technical innovations have not rendered them obsolete, especially since they can be rechanneled for widescreen and stereophonic sound and advertised as such. And, of course, with the nostalgia boom, many original films are drawing at the boxoffice again.

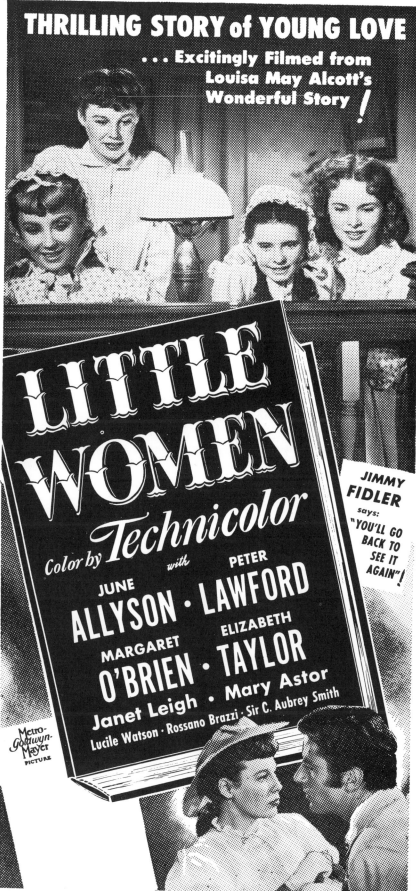

THRILLING STORY of YOUNG LOVE

...Excitingly Filmed from Louisa May Alcott's Wonderful Story!

LITTLE WOMEN

Color by *Technicolor*

with

JUNE **ALLYSON** · PETER **LAWFORD**

MARGARET **O'BRIEN** · ELIZABETH **TAYLOR**

Janet Leigh · Mary Astor

Lucile Watson · Rossano Brazzi · Sir C. Aubrey Smith

Metro-Goldwyn-Mayer PICTURE

JIMMY **FIDLER** says: "YOU'LL GO BACK TO SEE IT AGAIN"!

BETH MEG

AMY LAURIE

A New Sensation of Sheer Loveliness Glorifies the Screen!

Katharine **HEPBURN**

in America's best-loved romance

LITTLE WOMEN

by LOUISA MAY ALCOTT

with

**JOAN BENNETT
PAUL LUKAS
FRANCES DEE
JEAN PARKER**
Edna May Oliver
Douglass Montgomery
Henry Stephenson

AUNT MARCH MR. LAURENCE

Directed by GEORGE CUKOR.
MERIAN C. COOPER, executive
producer. Kenneth Macgowan,
associate producer.
RKO-RADIO PICTURE

RADIO CITY
MUSIC HALL
SHOWPLACE OF THE NATION

Let's Make It Again

Reissues have been big business time and again during industry history. A favorite practice is to reissue two films starring the same actor and feature them in a double bill. Clint Eastwood films and Sean Connery's James Bond movies are good recent examples of this. At other times, if an actor receives an Academy Award, some of his old films may be reissued and the advertising will exploit the Oscar.

Frequently, a supporting player will receive star billing in a reissue to capitalize on his or her current superstar status. Lana Turner was used to sell *They Won't Forget* in ads for that reissued Mervyn LeRoy film, although she did not have a starring role. The same is true for Humphrey Bogart in *Dead End* and *Black Legion*. Marilyn Monroe was used to sell the reissue of *The Asphalt Jungle*, despite the fact that she was on screen in the John Huston picture for only a few moments.

Certain films which have become screen classics—Chaplin movies, or *King Kong*—warrant special reissue campaigns. The ads are updated utilizing modern art design and ad copy.

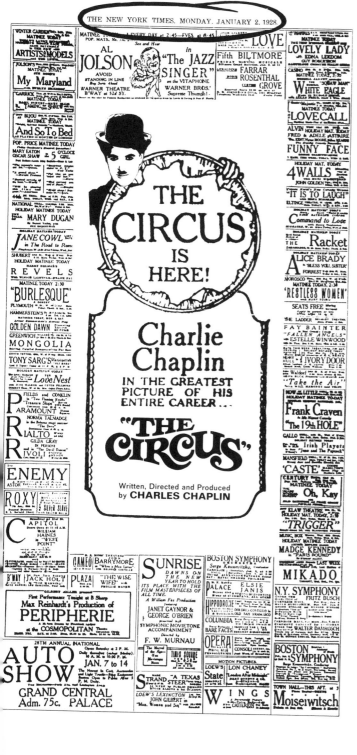

Films such as *City Lights* and
African Queen had successful reissue campaigns.

The musical story that fills the world with love.

He is a shy schoolmaster. She is a music hall star.
They marry and immediately have 283 children...all boys!

"The surprise hit
of sexy '69
will be an
old fashioned
love story,
'Goodbye,
Mr. Chips'"
—Look Magazine

Metro-Goldwyn-Mayer Presents
An Arthur P. Jacobs Production starring

Peter O'Toole · Petula Clark
"Goodbye, Mr. Chips"

co-starring **Sir Michael Redgrave**
Screenplay by Terence Rattigan
Directed by Herbert Ross
Produced by Arthur P. Jacobs
Music and Lyrics by Leslie Bricusse
Based on the Novel by James Hilton
Panavision® and Metrocolor

Original soundtrack album available on
MGM records, 8 track tape and cassettes.
Printed music from Hasting Music Corp.

Walt Disney Productions has always occupied a special place in the film industry as well as in the field of movie advertising. Today that is true to a greater degree than ever before.

Many of the changes that have occurred within the industry in general, and affected the way in which movies are sold, caused only a small ripple at Disney. The decline of the star system and the emergence of TV have not caused Disney the problems experienced by MGM, 20th Century-Fox and most of the other major companies. Unlike most of the other majors, Disney has not had to weather monumental financial storms. The swiftly changing tastes of today's movie public have, generally, provided few problems for Disney. In short, Disney is, as always, a part of the industry but still apart from it.

Undoubtedly, the prime reason for Disney's ability to remain impervious to the havoc experienced by the rest of the industry is the distinctive nature of its product. A Disney film is, with rare exception, immediately recognizable, whether it is a cartoon, a documentary or a live action re-creation of a classic. All are quality productions. Stars are not, and were never, considered particularly significant. Emphasis is on perfecting the technical aspects of the product, and vast sums of money are allocated toward this end.

Disney, unlike its studio counterparts, has always had one specific target audience. Its films have always been made to appeal to family tastes. From the beginning, the company, under the guiding hand of its founder Walt Disney, understood the importance of maintaining its image as a firm that would provide only the most wholesome type of entertainment. Of course there were great advantages to this approach. The company could be fairly sure that there would always be a ready market for its products. It did not have to concern itself with catching trends as did the other studios. The censorship difficulties encountered at other companies were unheard of at Disney. And most important, the timelessness of many of Disney's films meant that most of them could be re-released every five or seven years to take advantage of a new generation of children ready to be weaned on Snow White, Pinocchio et al.

At a time when most studios have grown accustomed to a continuous series of financial crises, Disney remains a veritable money machine. Several factors contribute to the company's financial strength. Since it has never relied on stars and, by industry standards, total budget costs are small, Disney is seldom vulnerable to the financial calamities common to studios which have to cover high fixed costs before films can turn a profit. Of the seven or eight productions released annually by the Disney organization, about half are usually re-releases. Therefore, except for advertising and other related costs, the money earned by these films represents pure profit as their production expenditures already have been covered. Disney has another advantage not usually available to other moviemakers. The company is able to parlay the popularity of many of its family-oriented films and its cartoon characters into rich sources of additional income. Other companies are able to capitalize on specific films but at Disney the efforts are devoted to merchandising

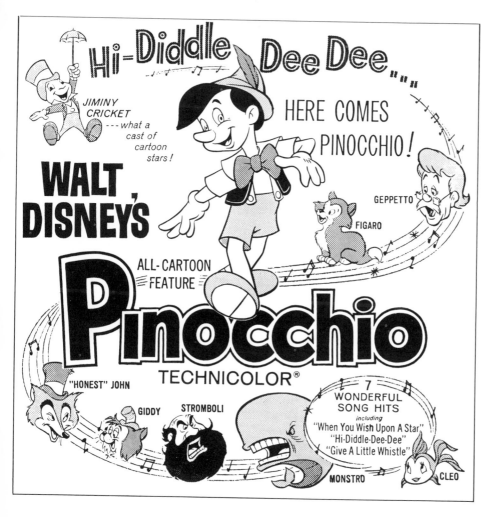

an entire concept. From record albums to Disneyland, the objective is to promote the image of Disney as the creator of family entertainment.

Since Disney's films can usually be counted on to be hits (of course, there have been exceptions, but the flops have never been expensive enough to cause a dent in the Disney economy), the company enjoys a good relationship with exhibitors. Generally, the company is able to win more favorable terms in regard to bookings, percentages, etc., than other distribution companies.

While most of the industry has suffered as a result of television's popularity, Disney has used the medium to its advantage. The Disney network program has proven a lucrative source of additional income while reinforcing the company image. It has added to the company's growth by introducing the Disney product to millions of children who might never have had the opportunity to see a Disney film.

Disney's method of advertising has undergone few changes over the years. While other studios have abandoned the practice of in-house staffs, Disney continues to do all its own campaigns. On a number of occasions the company has commissioned independent advertising agencies to create ads but the company has always decided that its own staff is capable of doing as good a job—if not better.

In comparison to the huge staffs that competing studios maintained at one time, Disney has always relied on a relatively small group (approximately 20 people) at Buena Vista Distribution Company, a subsidiary of Walt Disney Productions Inc., to handle the full range of activities involved in selling a movie. In contrast to the heavy turnover of personnel experienced at many other companies, Buena Vista's staff has a long record of service with the company. Consequently, all are knowledgeable about the nuances that go to make The Disney Look.

START 1970 WITH WALT DISNEY PRODUCTIONS and you'll start the year with big boxoffice grosses!

The giant of animated entertainment is back... More fantastically exciting, more magically in tune with today!

WALT DISNEY'S FANTASIA

TECHNICOLOR

Re-Released by Buena Vista Distribution Co., Inc. © Walt Disney Productions

HI-VOLTAGE HI-LARITY

A college sophomore crosses wires with a computer... and electrifies the establishment!

ALL NEW

WALT DISNEY productions'

the COMPUTER wore tennis shoes
TECHNICOLOR

STARRING
KURT RUSSELL · CESAR ROMERO · JOE FLYNN

Released by BUENA VISTA DISTRIBUTION CO., INC. © 1969 Walt Disney Productions

WALT DISNEY productions

It's a Love-In for Herbie ...the little car who shifts for himself!

THE LOVE BUG
"Herbie"

DEAN JONES · MICHELE LEE · DAVID TOMLINSON · BUDDY HACKETT
as Tennessee Steinmetz
JOE FLYNN · BENSON FONG · ANDY GRANATELLI · BILL WALSH and DON DaGRADI
BILL WALSH · ROBERT STEVENSON TECHNICOLOR

LOOK TO THE NAME WALT DISNEY FOR THE FINEST IN FAMILY ENTERTAINMENT [G] Suggested for General Audiences.

Walt Disney

The Disney organization has always excelled in the area of exploitation, and continues to emphasize this approach in selling a movie, though the use of exploitation has declined throughout the rest of the industry. The extensive coverage Disney gives to tie-ins can be illustrated by several of the examples in the pressbook for *Sleeping Beauty,* which was reissued in 1970. The tie-ins available to exhibitors were divided into three separate categories—toys, games and playthings ; housewares, stationery and miscellaneous ; and wearing apparel and soft goods. Among the products were novelty hats, jigsaw puzzles, Disney records, school lunch kits, toothpaste, infant garments and sweatshirts.

In addition to local tie-ins, exhibitors often have the benefit of national campaigns launched by major American companies like Kalcan, the pet food manufacturer, Kleenex, Sunmaid Raisins and Nabisco.

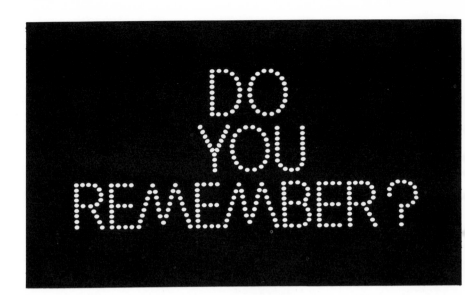

WOMEN WERE HIS IDOLS! MONEY WAS HIS GOD!

Revelling, fighting, marching with the mighty surge of America, they flamed in gaudy glory through the wildest, wickedest city on earth ... these fabulous "robber barons" of the realm of Rule-or-Ruin ...building railroad empires by day, and flinging away their lives and fortunes on Pleasure's darlings by night!

At last—the blazing romance of glamorous Josie Mansfield and flashing Jim Fisk ...reckless titan who battled his way to a throne of cornered gold, then madly danced with his love down the primrose path to Black Friday ...The screen sensation of a decade, played by a galaxy of stars in a hell-bent world of wine and women!

EDWARD ARNOLD
CARY GRANT · JACK OAKIE
FRANCES FARMER
in
"THE TOAST
OF NEW YORK"

Directed by
Rowland V. Lee

An Edward Small
Production

An RKO Radio Picture

Don't judge her by the way she looks

or by the things she's done to her Sister!

THERE ARE TWO SIDES TO EVERY STORY—AND EVERY WOMAN!

IDA
LUPINO
DENNIS
MORGAN
JOAN
LESLIE

Supported by
JACK CARSON
GLADYS GEORGE
FAYE EMERSON · Directed by
VINCENT SHERMAN
Screen Play by Daniel Fuchs and Peter Viertel
&
BUY WAR BONDS AND STAMPS
AT YOUR THEATRE

"The Hard Way"
A Great
WARNER BROS.
Picture!

Have you noticed that most of the swell shows
these days are produced by WARNERS!

"EVEN NOW SHE STOOD BETWEEN US...
THE TAUNT OF HER SMILE
LIKE A BLACK CURSE
ON OUR LOVE!"

In his arms, a girl of glorious love ... In his mind, a girl of terrible fascination!

SCREEN'S MOST GRIPPING DRAMA   OF MURDER...AND DESIRE!

ALICE FAYE
DANA ANDREWS
LINDA DARNELL
in
FALLEN ANGEL

with
Charles BICKFORD · Anne REVERE · Bruce CABOT
John CARRADINE · Percy KILBRIDE
Screen Play by Harry Kleiner · Based on the Novel by Marty Holland
Song "Slowly" by David Raksin and Kermit Goell
Produced and Directed by
OTTO PREMINGER
A 20th CENTURY-FOX PICTURE

FINISH THE JOB! BUY YOUR VICTORY LOAN BONDS AT YOUR FAVORITE THEATRE

BETTE DAVIS and CHARLES BOYER!

From the matchless pages of this brilliant best-seller comes a new chapter in film achievement! With all the incomparable artistry at their command these two great stars bring to life the deep emotions that stirred from every exciting word of the story!

You'll say when you see her that "Henriette" is a role heaven-sent just for Bette Davis! And you'll know, too, why Charles Boyer had to return all the way from France to play the impassioned Duc. For so many reasons this is the drama to be ranked in your memory with the topmost of all!

Included in the notable supporting cast are
JEFFREY LYNN · BARBARA O'NEIL
Virginia Weidler · Henry Daniell
Walter Hampden · George Coulouris
AN ANATOLE LITVAK PRODUCTION
Screen Play by Casey Robinson · Music by Max Steiner
A Warner Bros.-First National Picture

Warner Bros.
ARE HONORED TO OFFER
'ALL THIS AND
HEAVEN TOO'
FROM THE WORLD APPLAUDED NOVEL BY
Rachel Field

309

Do You Remember?

Fan Magazines

The advertising used in fan magazines was characterized by a very personal approach to the reader. The ads assumed the reader was a filmgoer. Thus, it was not unusual to find a single advertisement plugging as many as four movies. There was no fear of diluting the effect since the technique presupposed that the reader would attend as many films as he could.

The studios knew that fan magazines were not read and discarded immediately. The typical movie buff read and re-read the magazine.

In addition, the magazines were staples in beauty shops, barbershops, office waiting rooms, etc.

The ads in fan magazines usually emphasized the stars, since the magazines themselves were oriented toward this concept. The ad for *Don't Bother To Knock* with Marilyn Monroe as the focal point is a good illustrations of this technique.

The ad for *The Sullivans* is interesting because the picture was proving to be a flop until the title was changed to *The Fighting Sullivans*.

Fan Quiz

Special ads like the quiz below usually ran in fan magazines, but sometimes found their way into other print media. Feature story-like ads were used in all areas of advertising and offered the added attraction of appearing to be editorial rather than sales copy. Instead of hard sell, they tried to provide the reader with a bit of enjoyment and information.

This particular type of ad was specifically designed for the movie buff (referred to as movie fans in those days). The advertiser correctly assumed that the reader was familiar with the topic and receptive to his pitch. Note that in these ads not one specific film is advertised, but the emphasis was on films in general.

ONCE SHE WAS TOO HUNGRY
FOR LOVE...TO BE AFRAID!

...but now — it
was too late!

"I know what
you have done to
other women — and
what you will do to me,
But I don't care!"

Universal-International presents

JOAN CRAWFORD · JEFF CHANDLER
Female on the Beach

CO-STARRING
JAN STERLING with CECIL KELLAWAY · CHARLES DRAKE · JUDITH EVELYN · NATALIE SCHAFER
Directed by JOSEPH PEVNEY · Screenplay by ROBERT HILL and RICHARD ALAN SIMMONS · Produced by ALBERT ZUGSMITH

Ad Mat No. 403—600 Lines 10¾" x 4 col.

Press Books

Pressbooks (or Showman's Manuals, which is the term preferred by distributors) are selling tools provided by the distributor for local exhibitors. They are sales manuals showing the exhibitor how to sell the movie.

Pressbooks are divided into three sections: Advertising, Publicity and Promotion.

As the industry grew in the 1920's and '30's, the major studios began making their pressbooks more and more elaborate. But in the late '50's and '60's, pressbooks became thinner, were relegated to black and white and, with a few exceptions, were generally considered insignificant. True, they still carried the ads which were used by local exhibitors, but their publicity and exploitation sections were minimal.

The feature stories provided in the publicity section had been easy to plant in newspapers in the early days but now only small local newspapers might carry them.

The pressbook carries suggestions for promotional tie-ins and exploitation ideas for local exhibitors. In addition, the manual is meant to impress the exhibitor with the idea that the motion picture company intends to do everything possible to help make the picture a success.

In studio heydays, elaborate promotional and exploitation "kits" accompanied the pressbooks. Universal was usually credited with providing the most complete and effective pressbooks.

JOAN CRAWFORD HIGHLIGHTS NATIONAL DRAPERY CAMPAIGN

Newspaper Ads

With an ad in an early issue of Good Housekeeping Magazine as a send-off, the manufacturers of the famous Vogue Fibreglass draperies, have prepared an extensive advertising campaign featuring Joan Crawford and her picture FEMALE ON THE BEACH. The advertising is for the manufacturer's boucle drapery or curtain material which is woven of fibre-glass and arousing great interest among home-makers and decorators from coast to coast. Reproduced above are the three entirely different newspaper ad mats available to dealers. Note how the two column ad on the left makes a direct pitch for the picture. The other two are slightly off size mats making them suitable for use in a department store's general ad, or

as individuals. To the right is illustrated the easel-back display card suitable for windows and counters. This card has a mounted 8x10 print of a scene still from the picture. Through the full page trade ad, lower left, every drapery and curtain store and department store has been made familiar with the campaign. The ad appears in the June issue of Drapery and Curtain Department Magazine. The famous Owens - Corning Company, manufacturers of Fibreglass, now have in preparation a companion campaign. We suggest that you contact the local representative for details. For names of the local Vogue curtain outlet and for additional information, address

This Is Display Card →

Mr. Stuart Robertson

Robertson Factories, Inc.
42 Adams Street, Taunton, Mass.

AMERICAN GAS ASSOCIATION WILL PLACE ADS

The above still will be used as the basis for the AGA's four column, twelve inch (700 lines) ad which will be sent to all its member companies.

The 12,000 members of the AGA, each one interested in selling more gas and gas appliances, will go all out to help you sell this picture. The AGA was quick to realize that every woman who sees the picture will want an all gas kitchen and so have set up these tie-in plans. A 700 line ad with the still at the left as a basis will be distributed to all members to run in conjunction with your playdate. Proofs of the ad will be distributed for use as window displays. Members will also be urged to conduct cooking contests tied in with newspaper; to hold cooking school demonstration in theatre, if practical; to give away gas appliances as door or contest prizes (range and built-in oven, refrigerator), with eye-stopping lobby display in advance; arrange with builder of model home for installation of all gas modern kitchen with tie-in to picture; stage a "Fashions For Cooks" show with department store; to contact you so as to take full advantage of your showmanship, know-how and experience. The AGA Promotion Bureau in New York will be supplied with all dates on the picture and will in turn advise member companies.

LUSTRE CREME AD STARS LA CRAWFORD

Reproduced herewith is a full page ad for Lustre-Creme Shampoo which stars Joan Crawford and credits the picture FEMALE ON THE BEACH. Local dealers have been provided with special displays and banners for local promotion. Tie-in with the dealers for a bigger campaign by providing them with stills and other advertising material. Because of the variety and number of stores selling this product, it would be advantageous to contact the dealers before the play date so that you can take advantage of every promotion opportunity. This full color ad appears in Life, Ladies Home Journal, McCall's, Seventeen, True Story Women's Group and Dell Unit.

Page 4

GENEVA CABINETS IN BIG PROMOTION

The manufacturers of Geneva Cabinets have prepared special newspaper ad mats and window banners for local dealers. All this material credits FEMALE ON THE BEACH and will be distributed to their more than 3000 outlets. Notify the local dealer of the picture's play date at your theatre, and arrange to work closely with him for a well rounded campaign to augment your own promotional activities. Try and arrange for a free Geneva Kitchen Cabinet to be awarded as top prize in a contest as part of your campaign. For the name and address of the dealer in your area, contact:

Mr. J. G. Marshall

Geneva Modern Kitchens
Division of Acme Steel Company
Geneva, Illinois

SET OF 6 TIE-UP, 4 FASHION STILLS

Shown above are six carefully selected stills that should make it easy for you to grab some extra window displays as well as additional newspaper space. The merchandise featured are all items nationally advertised and distributed and local outlets should be happy to cooperate with you in your promotion plans. The items are: Revere Copper Ware; Roper Gas Range; Servel Refrigerator; Admiral TV sets; Ronson lighters and cameras (Rolleflex, or any other make). Also available but not shown are four fashion stills featuring Miss Crawford in her sensationally smart clothes. Order both sets direct from the

Exploitation Department
UNIVERSAL PICTURES COMPANY, INC.,
445 Park Ave., New York 22, N.Y.

The pressbook for *Female on the Beach* represents a good example of a typical, effective campaign. The distributor had something to work with—the stars—but the film certainly was not a pre-sold property based on a hit play or book.

In addition to the sample ads, publicity and promotion material, the pressbooks also told exhibitors what additional posters and accessories were available and how and why they should be used.

exploitation

24 SHEET STUNT

It has been a long time since a 24 sheet was so well adapted to the once off-used stunt of pasting it on the lobby floor. If you have a suitable corner for this purpose, the lower part of the walls could be decorated to represent a beach scene or the ocean beyond the beach.

If you do not have room to use the 24 sheet in the manner described above, we suggest that you build a sand box with the title as shown on the 24 sheet and have an attractive girl in a bathing suit lying in the sand. This would make an interesting advance display.

TITLE TIE-UPS

If you are playing this picture while the beach season is still on you have a wonderful opportunity to tie-up with local stores selling swim suits, beach wear, sun tan oil, beach umbrellas, etc., etc. Use the title of the picture to designate the various items.

TITLE SONG, RECORDS, BIG AIDS FOR YOUR CAMPAIGN

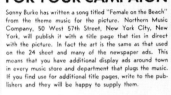

Sonny Burke has written a song titled "Female on the Beach" from the theme music for the picture. Northern Music Company, 50 West 57th Street, New York City, New York, will publish it with a title page that ties in direct with the picture. In fact the art is the same as that used on the 24 sheet and many of the newspaper ads. This means that you have additional display ads around town in every music store and department that plugs the music. If you find use for additional title pages, write to the publishers and they will be happy to supply them.

DECCA, CORAL, VICTOR RECORDS

In addition to the above you have further promotional possibilities on this song through recordings by Victor Young for Decca, Georgie Auld for Coral, and Leo Diamond for RCA Victor. This means that not only can you get more displays, but by supplying the various local disc jockeys with copies of the record, you can get the title on the air and possibly mention of your play date.

PHOTO PROMOTION . . . . . .

The title "Female on the Beach" is a natural for the tried and proved newspaper circulation stunt of the circled photograph. In this case, photographer roams the local beaches, photographing groups of girls. The newspaper publishes one of the pictures each day with a circle around the head of one of the girls. When she comes to the newspaper or theatre to identify herself, she is presented with certain prizes or gifts. Of course, in order for this to be practical your play date must be before the beach season opens. However, should you be playing the picture later in the year, the same idea could probably be used by photographing girls in the local resort wear departments and shops.

TEASER TRAILER

Give *importance* to your playdate by using this teaser trailer one week in advance of the regular trailer! Build up anticipation of great entertainment to come by using the teaser first . . . then complete the job with your regular trailer! To help build your campaign for "Female on the Beach," U-I provides this teaser trailer FREE. Order direct from your Universal Exchange.

FREE AT ALL UNIVERSAL BRANCHES

RADIO MATERIAL for VISUAL and AUDIO AIR CAMPAIGN TV

TV TRAILERS -- FREE

A set of TV spots have been prepared with a variety of selling angles that highlight the great dramatic qualities of "Female on the Beach." TV trailer spots are printed on 16 millimeter film, each built with top showmanship values. Order free of charge from Jeff Livingston, Eastern Ad Manager, Universal Pictures Co., Inc., 445 Park Avenue, New York 22, New York. Please specify name and address of station on which you plan to use trailers.

TELOP or SLIDE

Telop and Slide are available as shown. $5.00 without imprint. $7.50 with theatre name and playdate. $10.00 with theatre and station identification, only on the Telop. State whether you want Slide or Telop. Order from QQ Title Card Co., 1243 Sixth Ave., New York, N. Y.

Suggested 'Live' Audio for Use With 'Telop' or Slide

ANNOUNCER: Fear and fascination in a masterpiece of suspense . . . . see Joan Crawford, Jeff Chandler with Jan Sterling in FEMALE ON THE BEACH.

FREE RADIO SPOT TRANSCRIPTION

This platter records EIGHT SPOTS, each a showman's pitch to sell "Female on the Beach." There are two 1-minute, two 30-second, two 20-second, two 15-second spots. All allow time for theatre signature. In ordering be sure to mention title of the picture. Order from Radio Department, Universal-International Studios, Universal City, California.

RADIO INTERVIEW RECORD WITH *Joan Crawford*

A five minute open-end personalized platter of questions and answers which provides the effect of a studio interview. An accompanying script supplies the questions which your local announcer asks. Answers to each question have been transcribed by Joan Crawford on the platter, providing the effect of a live studio interview. Order from Radio Dept., Universal-International Studios, Universal City, California.

SUGGESTED COPY FOR LIVE RADIO SPOTS

(1 Minute)
ANNOUNCER: There's something about a beach . . . maybe the moonlight . . . or the violence of the waves . . . that can get under a woman's skin . . . and when a woman is too rich . . . and too lonely to care . . . anything can happen . . . and in FEMALE ON THE BEACH . . . well plenty happens . . . See Joan Crawford and Jeff Chandler with co-star Jan Sterling in FEMALE ON THE BEACH . . . the story of a woman's hunger for a man . . . so powerful that nothing else mattered . . . not even what he was . . . or what he might do to her . . . or the price she must pay . . . See Joan Crawford as Lynn Markham, rich, beautiful and bored . . . her magnetism a challenge to Jeff Chandler as Drummy Hall, tall charming beach drifter who collected women for a living . . . what happened was bound to happen . . . there was no escape . . . see FEMALE ON THE BEACH . . . fear and fascination in a masterpiece of suspense . . . starring Joan Crawford, Jeff Chandler and Jan Sterling . . . with Cecil Kellaway, Charles Drake, Judith Evelyn and Natalie Schafer . . . FEMALE ON THE BEACH.

(30 Seconds)
ANNOUNCER: She was rich, beautiful and much too lonely to care what happened to her . . . until she met Drummy and found out what could happen . . . only then it was too late . . . see Joan Crawford, Jeff Chandler in FEMALE ON THE BEACH . . . co-starring Jan Sterling . . . never has a woman loved so deeply . . . or so dangerously . . . she knew what he was . . . and she was afraid . . . yet every fibre of her being cried out for him . . . he was the kind of man that her kind of woman can't leave alone . . . SEE FEMALE ON THE BEACH.

(15 Seconds)
ANNOUNCER: Joan Crawford, Jeff Chandler with Jan Sterling in FEMALE ON THE BEACH . . . the story of a woman's hunger for a man . . . so powerful that nothing else mattered . . . not even what he was . . . what he might do to her . . . or the price she must pay . . . see FEMALE ON THE BEACH.

Page 5

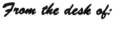

Turnaround Campaigns

New ad campaigns are frequently developed after a film has opened, and the initial response is disappointing. Within the industry this move is referred to as a "turnaround campaign."

With a "Turn-around," simply stated the producer is hoping to turn his flop film into a hit. However, it is generally conceded that a new ad campaign alone cannot save a film. The movie itself must have some intrinsic merit.

The boxoffice history of the film *The Mark,* which is often cited as a successful "turnaround," illustrates this point. The movie relate the story of a rehabilitated child molester who falls in love

A film which doesn't 'protect' you from the truth!

JIM FULLER: He was searching for his manhood.

RUTH: She gave him more than herself.

DOC McNALLY: He was constantly pointing the direction.

MARIA SCHELL
STUART WHITMAN
in "**THE MARK**"
and ROD STEIGER
as Doc McNally

with BRENDA de BANZIE DONALD WOLFIT · Directed by Guy Green
A Raymond Stross—Sidney Buchman Production
A Continental Distributing Inc. Release

with a woman who has a young daughter. When his past is revealed the couple suffers a great deal of anguish.

The film handled the difficult subject with taste and discretion and the acting of Stuart Whitman and Maria Schell was superb. The ads for the film prior to its opening practically ignored the plot, and generated little excitement or interest.

However, when the film received excellent reviews, the advertising campaign became more dynamic. The new ads were forthright about the plot and were far more provocative. The film became a success.

It is doubtful whether the new ad campaign could have effected such an outcome without the benefit of good reviews and an excellent film to begin with.

SENSATIONALISM BE DAMNED... HERE'S THE TRUTH ABOUT "THE MARK."

Because "THE MARK" deals with themes that are, to say the least, touchy, we were a little reluctant to discuss it frankly. We were more than hesitant to tell the story in our advertisements for fear of being accused of "sensationalism." And so we thought in vague general terms about the picture and its high quality. Now, sensationalism be damned, we want to be truthful and fair to this very uncommon film. What's it about? In five words, it's about a victim of sexual deviation. You follow him through psychiatry through group therapy, through his tenuous meetings with women—and finally the one woman who takes him across the threshold—into manhood. The words are blunt and dramatic. And they're words you don't have to be a psychiatrist to understand. At the expense of a blush, or even a moment's discomfort, why don't you make an appointment with "THE MARK"?

MARIA SCHELL
STUART WHITMAN
ROD STEIGER
"THE MARK"
A Continental
Distributing, Inc Release

THE MARK